CHRISTOPHER HARDING

# A Short History of Japan

A PELICAN BOOK

PELICAN
*an imprint of*
PENGUIN BOOKS

# PELICAN BOOKS

UK | USA | Canada | Ireland | Australia
India | New Zealand | South Africa

Pelican Books is part of the Penguin Random House group of companies
whose addresses can be found at global.penguinrandomhouse.com

Penguin Random House UK
One Embassy Gardens, 8 Viaduct Gardens, London SW11 7BW

penguin.co.uk

 Penguin
Random House
UK

First published in Great Britain by Pelican Books 2025
001

Book design by Matthew Young
Set in 11/16.13pt FreightText Pro
Typeset by Jouve (UK), Milton Keynes
Printed and bound in Great Britain by Clays Ltd, Elcograf S.p.A.

The authorized representative in the EEA is Penguin Random House Ireland,
Morrison Chambers, 32 Nassau Street, Dublin DO2 YH68

A CIP catalogue record for this book is available from the British Library

ISBN: 978-0-241-56319-9

Penguin Random House is committed to a sustainable future
for our business, our readers and our planet. This book is made from
Forest Stewardship Council® certified paper.

# Contents

Japan and the Korean Peninsula

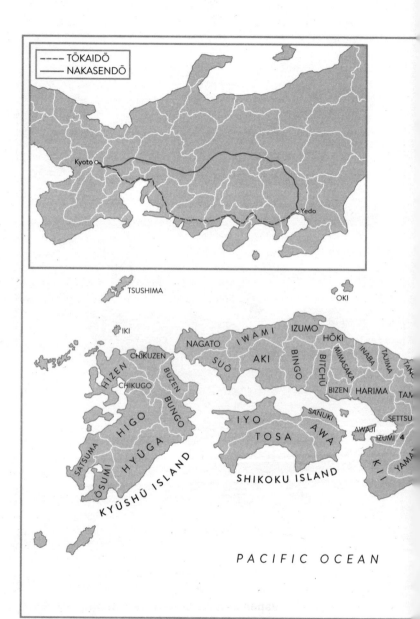

TŌKAIDŌ
NAKASENDŌ

Kyoto
Yedo

TSUSHIMA

OKI

IKI

NAGATO

IWAMI

IZUMO

HŌKI

CHIKUZEN

SUŌ

AKI

BINGO

BITCHŪ

MIMASAKA

INABA

TAJIMA

TANG

HIZEN

CHIKUGO

BUZEN

BIZEN

HARIMA

TAM

HIGO

BUNGO

IYO

SANUKI

AWAJI

SETTSU

SATSUMA

ŌSUMI

HYŪGA

TOSA

AWA

IZUMI

4

KII

YAMA

SHIKOKU ISLAND

KYŪSHŪ ISLAND

PACIFIC OCEAN

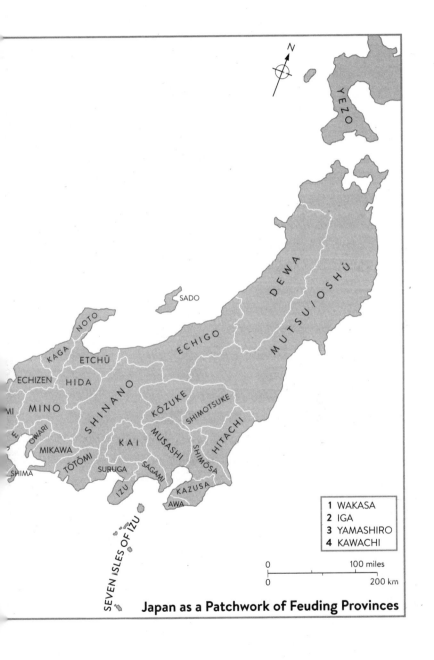

**Japan as a Patchwork of Feuding Provinces**

YEZO

SADO

DEWA

MUTSUIOSHŪ

NOTO

ECHIGO

KAGA

ETCHŪ

ECHIZEN

HIDA

SHINANO

KŌZUKE

SHIMOTSUKE

MINO

HITACHI

OWARI

KAI

MUSASHI

MIKAWA

SHIMŌSA

TŌTŌMI

SURUGA

SAGAMI

SHIMA

IZU

KAZUSA

AWA

SEVEN ISLES OF IZU

| 1 | WAKASA |
| 2 | IGA |
| 3 | YAMASHIRO |
| 4 | KAWACHI |

0       100 miles

0       200 km

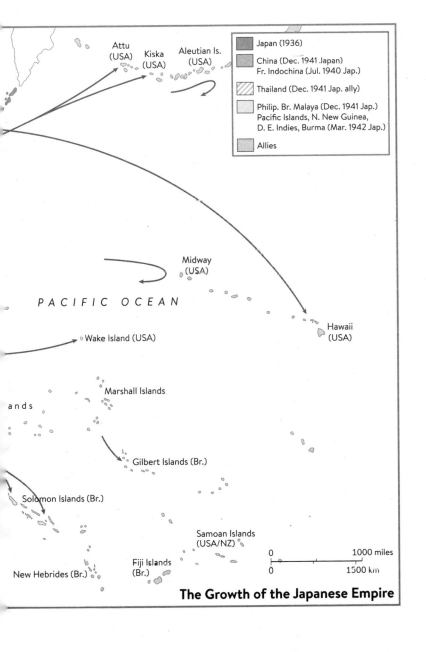

| | Japan (1936) |
|---|---|
| | China (Dec. 1941 Japan) Fr. Indochina (Jul. 1940 Jap.) |
| | Thailand (Dec. 1941 Jap. ally) |
| | Philip. Br. Malaya (Dec. 1941 Jap.) Pacific Islands, N. New Guinea, D. E. Indies, Burma (Mar. 1942 Jap.) |
| | Allies |

Attu (USA)
Kiska (USA)
Aleutian Is. (USA)

Midway (USA)

PACIFIC OCEAN

Wake Island (USA)

Hawaii (USA)

Marshall Islands

ands

Gilbert Islands (Br.)

Solomon Islands (Br.)

Samoan Islands (USA/NZ)

New Hebrides (Br.)
Fiji Islands (Br.)

| 0 | | 1000 miles |
|---|---|---|
| 0 | | 1500 km |

**The Growth of the Japanese Empire**

Japan's Prefectures (present day)

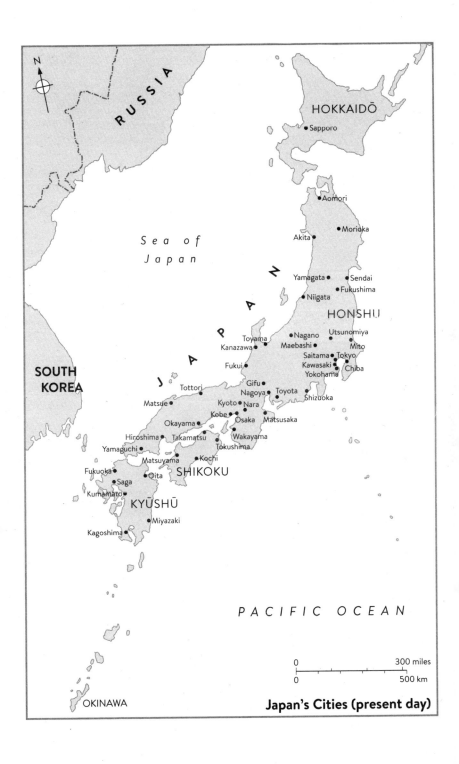

**Japan's Cities (present day)**

# Introduction

A Japanese passport will get you into 194 countries and regions around the world, visa-free. Only a Singapore passport beats it, at 195. And yet, fewer than 20 per cent of people in Japan own a passport, compared with almost 85 per cent in the UK. One of the biggest reasons given for shunning foreign travel is geography. Why go abroad when the 3,000-kilometre-long Japanese archipelago offers such an extraordinary diversity of climate, from the Siberian north down to the sub-tropical south?

Holiday-makers seeking the romance of boreal forests and icy lakes need go no further than Hokkaidō, the northernmost of Japan's four main islands. Skiers head there, too, celebrating the town of Niseko as the 'powder capital of the world'. To Hokkaidō's south lies Honshū, the largest and most populous island in the archipelago, and the engine-house of its history. Tectonic plates grinding away beneath have left Honshū divided down the middle by a mountainous spine and spurs. Most people live on the island's temperate, fertile plains, in modern megacities like Tokyo and Osaka, heading into the mountains when they want to ski, hike or soak in a natural hot-spring bath.

Japan's third main island, Shikoku, can be found tucked

into Honshū's lower belly, while the fourth, Kyūshū, lies just to the south-west. Japanese tourists love both for their dramatic scenery, hot springs, beaches and food. The diversity of Japan's climate, combined with strong regional identities, has yielded a culinary culture that prizes local seasonal produce and simple preparation. Kagawa prefecture in Shikoku regards itself as the best place to go in Japan for udon – thick noodles made from wheat. Kyūshū is famous for its Hakata tonkotsu ramen, served in a cloudy broth made by boiling pork bones for hour upon hour.

Anyone in search of surfing, scuba-diving or the white sands of a tropical paradise will head still further along the archipelago's gentle south-western curve to the island chain of Okinawa – the westernmost of which, Yonaguni, sits within view, on a clear day, of Taiwan.

The chance to enjoy all this via fast and efficient transport, staying in accommodation where levels of cleanliness and service are dependably high and with people who speak your language and share with you a basic set of assumptions about how to treat one another has helped to turn domestic tourism in Japan into a multi-trillion-yen industry. By contrast, incoming tourists, particularly to traditional cultural centres like Kyoto, are fast gaining a reputation for being insensitive and even rather boorish, failing to understand what is required of good guests.

Critics of Japan look at low levels of passport ownership, a muted role in international affairs – despite being a major world economy – and a vexed debate about immigration, and diagnose a classic case of island mentality. Here is a place, they suggest, that is confident in its own virtues and cautious, even suspicious, in its dealings with the outside world. There is some truth to this. Where landlocked countries have to constantly learn to live with their neighbours, come what may, Japan is separated from the eastern edge of Eurasia by a narrow stretch of water – the Sea of Japan – and from the Americas by the vast Pacific Ocean. Neither is an impermeable barrier, but both have allowed Japan's rulers, across the centuries, to exercise a degree of control over the people and ideas making their way into the archipelago.

The filtering and creative adaptation of outside influence, combined with a seemingly never-ending struggle to knit the communities of the archipelago into a single whole, represent the central drama of Japanese history. It has so far played out in three great phases. Across the early centuries of recorded history, China and the kingdoms of the Korean peninsula supplied Japan with iron-working and rice cultivation, Buddhism and Confucianism, architecture and a writing system, rules, fashions and a wide range of arts, poetry prime among them. From the 1500s onwards, seafaring Europeans began to have an impact in Japan. Portuguese traders and Jesuit missionaries brought with them new wealth, weapons, goods, fashions and religious ideals, further enriching and complicating a period of exceptional innovation and turmoil in Japan. Finally, from the mid-1800s onwards, Japan was forced to find its place in a modern, industrialising world whose standards and values were set by the powerful economies of western Europe and North America.

The task of creating and sustaining a single, flourishing society on the Japanese archipelago has changed hands many times. Unity of a kind was first achieved in the early centuries CE, as the Yamato clan emerged as the paramount power on Honshū and claimed for its leaders the title of *tennō*, or 'Heavenly Sovereign'. These emperors and empresses enjoyed real political power only for a few centuries before warriors and later civilian politicians took control. Still, the culture of the imperial court, flourishing in Kyoto in the tenth and eleventh centuries, has continued to exert an impressive gravitational pull across the ensuing thousand years. Whatever their origins, aspiring leaders in Japan sought to immerse themselves in a suite of art forms that were East Asian in origin but Japanese in their perfection: poetry and calligraphy; painting and performance; the art of hospitality found in the tea ceremony.

A medieval warlord might shed blood by day and then by night pen a poem, dance a few steps from a Nō play or lose himself in the sound of a flute wafting on the wind from somewhere in his camp. Wealthy merchants in early modern Edo (now Tokyo) sought out bluffers' guides to Japanese high culture and some even had theatre stages built inside their homes. Into the modern age, as Japan was flooded with Western ideas and inventions, it found its place in the world both as an aggressive imperial power and as a source of rich and varied forms of culture, from ceramics and Zen to manga and sushi. It is a testament to the remarkable evolution and staying power of Japanese culture that court painting of Japan's classical Heian era and the piratical adventures of the hit manga *One Piece* – the second-best selling literary series in history after *Harry Potter* – form part of the same rich tapestry.

Part of the appeal of Japanese culture in the West has been an emphasis on rules, discipline and self-mastery in perfecting this or that art form. Anything ending in *dō*, meaning 'way', is a part of this world: from *judō*, the 'gentle way', to *chadō*, the way of tea. And yet these forms owe something of their beauty and sophistication to the insight that human attempts to control the world have their limits: a withered, weathered look is a prized aesthetic in a range of arts and crafts, while the *kintsugi* method of repairing broken pottery highlights and celebrates cracks with powdered gold or silver. Meanwhile, the price paid for Japan's inspiring and dramatic topography is a vulnerability to sudden tragedy: earthquakes, tsunamis, volcanic eruptions, typhoons and mudslides. The last big earthquake to hit Tokyo, in 1923, killed more than 100,000 people and was read by some at the time as a warning against modernity's hubris.

A sense of living at nature's whim underpins Shintō, 'the way of the gods' – that is, Japan's native religion – alongside a storytelling tradition that depicts the natural landscape as home to gods, goddesses and all manner of strange beings, some of whom one might fleetingly encounter at twilight, or on a lonely mountain pass. The Buddhist thread in Japanese history complements this with a keen sense of life's evanescence: an awareness that everything is constantly passing into existence and out again.

It would be an exaggeration to claim – and, indeed, unfair to expect – that everyone in Japan possesses a joined-up sense of this rich inheritance. But it is probably fair to say that memories of the past, often heavily idealised, have driven Japanese history onwards more frequently and with greater power than any utopian goal. The influence of Christianity, with its hope of future redemption, has never been strong in Japan. Shaping people's aspirations instead we find a Buddhist sense of cyclical time, an emphasis in Shintō on renewal and a Confucian respect for others and for the ways of one's forebears. One doesn't need to be schooled in any of these philosophies to feel their effects in everyday life in Japan: the foods and rituals of New Year; the celebration of youth and rebirth that accompanies cherry blossom season in the spring; the greeting of the dead at O-Bon in the summer.

Most people in Japan will also have a good sense of their history's A-listers: Murasaki Shikibu, author of *The Tale of Genji* in *c.* 1000 CE; Oda Nobunaga, warlord and unifier of Japan; Tokugawa Ieyasu, founder of a shogunate that kept Japan for the most part peaceful and stable across two centuries. Television and cinema have played their part in this across the modern era, from the first soundless samurai films of the 1920s through to the time-slip dramas of the twenty-first century – one of which features a slightly spoiled and lazy teenaged boy being transported back to Oda Nobunaga's time, there to learn what it means to be a man. Manga and anime carry the flame of Japanese history and culture, too: often the work of highly sophisticated artists who wear their learning lightly but weave into their stories some of the great figures, symbols and dilemmas of the past.

Manga and anime have become central, too, to how young people around the world encounter and come to fall in love with Japan and its history. The aim of this *Short History* is to offer a guide to the overall terrain, helping readers to connect their favourite people, products and moments to the bigger story of the archipelago. It is surely one of the most fertile places on earth for drama, big ideas, great tragedy, superb cuisine and creative achievements of all kinds. By the end, my hope is that readers will have come to sympathise a little with the 80 per cent of Japanese who don't feel the need for a passport. Why sign up for one when to stay at home is such an adventure?

# CHAPTER 1
## The First Communities

Some of the first people to arrive on the Japanese archipelago, *c.* 35,000 BCE in the western calendar, probably walked there. Until sea levels rose around 13,000 years ago, the archipelago was connected to the Asian mainland for long periods at a time via a northern land bridge running across from Siberia and a southern bridge from the Korean peninsula. Others most likely arrived via various sorts of watercraft, from dugout canoes to sturdy rafts. They settled in parts of what is now Hokkaidō, alongside the coastal plains of Honshū, down into Kyūshū and further south on some of the Okinawan islands. Life for these palaeolithic hunter-gatherers seems to have consisted of making sorties from temporary tent shelters to forage for food and hunt a combination of giant deer, Naumann's elephants and woolly mammoths. Their modest armoury included spears and arrows alongside edge-ground stone axes, excellent for felling trees and working with wood.

The first major epoch in the islands' human history lasted from around 14,500 BCE to 500 BCE. This era is called 'Jōmon' ('cord-marked'), after the rope-like patterning found on pottery unearthed from this period – some of the oldest pottery to have survived anywhere in the world. The earliest vessels were small and portable, perhaps modelled in size and design on woven baskets and used to store and cook food. As time went on they became larger and larger, suggesting a shift to a more sedentary culture, making use of caves and rock shelters in a way that their palaeolithic ancestors had not.

The transition to a more settled way of life seems to have coincided with the hunting to virtual extinction of big game, followed by a steadily warming climate. Both things helped to turn the peoples of the archipelago, by around 5000 BCE, from heavy meat-eaters into consumers primarily of seasonal plant life, much of which, including acorns, had to be boiled to render it safe and soft for consumption. People ate salmon, trout and shellfish, too. Jōmon skeletons have been found whose inner ears are partially protected by bone, suggesting that diving was a major part of life. They also ate the infamous puffer fish, the discerning of whose edible versus poisonous parts was presumably the result of some rather unpleasant trial and error. Boar, mountain bears, deer and smaller game could also be found on the menu, alongside swans, albatrosses, owls, wolves, rats, hares and flying squirrels. Dogs were used to help out during a hunt, and from the way they were buried they seem to have been held in a certain affection.

The second half of the Jōmon period, from roughly 2500 BCE, witnessed a rapid growth in the archipelago's population, some of whom began to live in small communities consisting of family pit-dwellings, around half a metre deep and three metres or so in width, with thatched roofs. These homes were arranged in a circle around land used for communal purposes, including the storage of food. Most of what was needed to live was close at hand: wood, water and food of all kinds. Trading and gift-giving with other communities meanwhile brought both necessities and luxuries into the home: combs, earrings and clothing made from hemp; lacquered vessels, produced by tapping the lacquer tree for its sap and mixing this with black and red pigmens; elaborately decorated pottery lamps for giving light after dark; and pots decorated with such a rich array of symbolic motifs that they may have been used in ritual or storytelling.

Did prehistoric Japanese have rhythm? Pots have been found, with holes around the rim, that suggest they did: it is thought that cords were run through these holes to secure animal skin across the top. Other objects have been found that may have served as musical instruments, from hollow vessels that make a sound when you blow into them to sets of shells capable of functioning as castanets. Some combination of these may well have been used in Jōmon rituals, of the kind suggested by pots discovered featuring appliquéd images of figures dancing with raised hands.

The meanings of these symbols are unclear, but there is strong evidence of a Jōmon concern with the presence in the landscape of powerful and perhaps personal forces. It is striking that people who were easily capable of making hunting tools and everyday goods with great precision nevertheless produced clay figurines that lacked heads or featured distorted physiognomies. Some have suggested that these are not so much poor or damaged representations of human beings as anthropocentric intuitions of mysterious beings.

Some of these figurines likely served in rituals relating to fertility, childbirth and burial, and were linked in turn to those forces or beings in the landscape. At a number of

Jōmon sites, if you stand in the middle of the settlement and look out over the graves you find a distant mountain directly in your line of sight. This suggests a precursor to the Shintō idea that spirits reside in great and impressive features of the landscape. Elsewhere on the archipelago there is evidence of burial locations and the orientation of graves being governed by the position of the sun in the sky at particular times of the day and year. Pottery motifs meanwhile suggest that the numbers three and five held particular significance for some in the late Jōmon period. Whether and why that might have been the case, we may never know.

For all the appearance of a varied menu and a settled life supported by a community and an array of tools and possessions, it was common in the Jōmon era not to live past one's mid-thirties. Food shortages and even famine were not unknown. All the more reason, then, why the introduction to the archipelago, around 500 BCE, of short-grain rice cultivation was so momentous. It most likely made its way there via migrants from Korea, crossing in large numbers from the peninsula to Kyūshū and spreading outwards from there – as with other cultural changes in this epoch, different parts of the archipelago were affected at different times.

These migrants brought iron tools, too: useful for clearing land for cultivation, bringing in the harvest and carving wood with greater efficiency and accuracy. The appearance of bronze bells, mirrors, daggers and other objects around the same time, alongside a growing population, suggest a new phase in the life of the archipelago. It has been given the name Yayoi, after a distinctive variety of pottery from the period that was first discovered in the Yayoi neighbourhood of modern-day Tokyo.

A few centuries into the Yayoi period, usually dated from 500 BCE to 250 CE, Chinese records furnish us with our earliest written accounts of life on the archipelago. The *Hou Han Shu* (*History of the Later Han*) and the *Wei Chih* (*Records of Wei*) together paint a picture of a place that by at least the early third century CE was home to around a hundred chiefdoms capable of imposing their will on their neighbours via a blend of warfare, economic pressure and what Chinese observers regarded as sorcery.

The most important of all these chiefdoms, in Chinese eyes at least, was Yamatai. Its location on the archipelago – Kyūshū versus Honshū – remains a matter of heated debate, and its ruler, Queen Himiko (*c*. 170 CE–*c*. 248 CE), the object of great fascination. The Chinese, with whom Himiko initiated an exchange of emissaries, used the unfortunate appellation *Wa*, meaning 'little people' or 'dwarfs', for inhabitants both of the southern part of the Korean peninsula and the archipelago. But they regarded Himiko with fear and respect. She was said to spend much of her time communing with the gods inside a heavily guarded castle, while a thousand maidservants tended to her needs and her younger brother took care of the day-to-day business of running Yamatai.

Himiko's world was one of large settlements – some of up to 2,000 people – and increasing hierarchy, in which a few elite households oversaw the specialised labour of the rest: farmers, potters, metal-workers and more. According to the *Wei Chih*, an aristocrat might have four or five wives, while a commoner made do with two or three. Those same commoners would retreat a step or two when an aristocrat walked by, crouching or kneeling on the floor if they wished to address him.

Hierarchy among the Wa seems to have been the product of surplus rather than scarcity. According to the *Wei Chih*, men and women alike wore loose, unstitched cloth – linen, silk and cotton were all available – and walked around barefoot thanks to a climate that was tolerably warm in summer and winter alike. They enjoyed vegetables, fish and alcoholic drinks, and were generally well-behaved: women were neither immoral nor envious, and theft was rare. This may have been because punishments for wrongdoing were so severe, ranging from the enslavement of a person's close relatives to the execution of their extended family. War appears to have been a frequent occurrence. Settlements were defended by stockades, moats, embankments and watchtowers, while warriors employed varying combinations of swords, spears and wooden bows firing iron- or bone-tipped bamboo arrows. Himiko perhaps hoped that, alongside gods and weapons, her Chinese connections would help to secure her chiefdom.

Chinese observers of Himiko's world either did not know the details of her 'sorcery' or thought the concept obvious enough as to require little elucidation. Thread-relief figures on bronze bells from this period show what looks like ecstatic dancing by a shaman holding a rod. Bells and mirrors appear to have been used, perhaps to the accompaniment of flutelike and zitherlike instruments whose remains have been found at various archaeological sites. Himiko herself may have been thought capable of calling up the spirits of the dead, and of engaging in divination and propitiation – essential for a chiefdom whose wealth and welfare depended on a rice crop that was vulnerable to the elements. The people of her chiefdom had their part to play, too: our Chinese texts note that they clapped and used fresh running water in their worship, perhaps as a means of ensuring ritual purity.

When Himiko died, around the year 248, she was buried beneath an impressive mound of earth some 145 metres in diameter. According to the *Wei Chih*, 'over a hundred male and female attendants followed her to the grave' and more than a thousand people died in the disorder that followed her passing. Whether or not these details can be relied on, it is clear from archaeological discoveries dating from around this time that the archipelago – and central parts of Honshū in particular – was passing into a period of ever-more impressive burial sites. They are thought to be the final resting places of rulers whose peoples placed them high above the ordinary run of men and women. The idea was beginning to emerge of a community led by people who did not just commune with the gods, but who claimed to be their sons and daughters.

# CHAPTER 2

# The Birth of 'Japan'

Spring has come when the mist trails
On the heaven-descended hill of Kagu,
The lake is rippled by the breezes through the pines
And cherry-flowers fill the leafy boughs.

The mallards call to their mates
Far off on the water,
And the teal cry and whirr
About the beach.

In the 700s CE, our picture of the archipelago begins to sharpen dramatically. Earlier centuries come to us in fragments of pottery, bone, stone and iron, alongside the observations of visitors from the Asian mainland. Now, in lines like the ones above, from an anthology of more than 4,000 poems called *Man'yōshū* (*Ten Thousand Leaves*, *c*. mid-700s), we encounter the people of the archipelago for the first time in their own words. We find relish of nature's gifts, sparingly expressed, and an interweaving of seasons, gods, landscapes and the lives of the poets – for many of whom courtship and romance are their most precious concerns.

Besides poetry, we have history. The oldest known texts to be produced in the archipelago are the *Kojiki* (*Record of Ancient Matters*, *c*. 712) and the *Nihon Shoki* (*Chronicles of*

*Japan, c.* 720). The latter focuses on the more or less sober, if not always strictly factual, recollection of salient moments and individuals, somewhat in the style of a Chinese chronicle. *Kojiki* runs broader, incorporating poetry, song, epic mythology and keen insights into the lives and attitudes of those who had, by this time, won a battle for the heartlands of Honshū.

That battle was fought across what has come to be called the Yamato period, stretching from 250 CE to 710 CE. It opened with the appearance of increasingly grand *kofun*, or 'ancient graves', in which great rulers were interred. Hollow clay figurines known as *haniwa*, some of which were several feet tall, were arrayed in parallel lines around the edges of these graves. According to the *Nihon Shoki*, these *haniwa* were used to replace the human attendants who were once buried upright in the top of rulers' tombs. The attendants' slow, hideous deaths – pecked and torn apart by ravens and dogs – came to be considered cruel and a bit unseemly. This may have been a tall story: there is no archaeological evidence for human sacrifice on the archipelago. Instead, *haniwa* were probably intended to express the beneficence of the deceased during their lifetime, or else to keep them company in the next world: while early *haniwa* were simple cylinders, later designs included shamans, wrestlers and musicians alongside dancers, birds and men armoured for war.

The best-known of the burial mounds is the Daisen Kofun, created in the mid-400s and located just south of today's city of Osaka. Almost 500 metres long and thirty-five metres high, it appears from far above as a circle embedded in the top of a slim triangle – giving it a keyhole shape – and it is surrounded by greenery and a triple moat. No one knows for certain who is interred here, but the Daisen Kofun is usually associated with a great ruler named Nintoku. By this time, a chiefdom located in the Yamato Basin in south-central Honshū was using a combination of alliances and horse-mounted warfare to extend its reach across central Honshū and down towards Kyūshū. Even in regions to which Yamato's suzerainty did not extend, the proliferation of *kofun* with their grave goods and associated rituals was a sign of an emerging, shared elite culture, out of which a state would one day be born.

By the early sixth century, Yamato's rulers had taken to styling themselves 'Great Sovereign' and were increasingly drawing on Chinese and Korean culture to help them consolidate and justify their growing power. Beginning in the late fifth or early sixth century, and largely via the Korean kingdom of Paekche, some of the Chinese Classics began to make their way into the archipelago. Paekche also provided the inspiration for the Yamato court's use of a system – known as *be* (pronounced 'bay') – for organising and managing craftspeople and suppliers of goods, from painters to fishermen. Clans (*uji*) began to form and prosper on the basis of their role in this burgeoning court bureaucracy, enjoying the right to administer and tax allotted areas of land. The danger for the Great Sovereigns, now and into the future, was that a rival clan might accrue power and wealth that approximated their own.

Buddhism, too, appears to have entered the archipelago via Paekche, most likely at some point in the mid-sixth century. If the account in the *Nihon Shoki* is to be believed, there followed a period of intense clan rivalry: between the Soga, as advocates for Buddhism and Korean culture in general, and the Mononobe, whose status and fortunes were tied to their role as ritualists in service to the islands' native gods. Violent clashes ensued in the 580s, out of which the Soga emerged victorious – and powerful enough to have one of their own, a woman named Suiko, installed as one of only a handful of female Great Sovereigns.

Temples now began to take over from tombs as portals between this world and the next. Many of the earliest were built in part by Korean hands: Buddhist monks who doubled as master craftsmen, capable of assembling great cavernous constructions of heavy wood with tiled roofs. Housed within were impressive sculptures and paintings of buddhas and bodhisattvas, around whom wafted incense and the sound of solemnly chanted prayers. Many of those prayers were said for the welfare of the realm: Buddhism's gradual acceptance in the Yamato kingdom depended on the idea that, far from giving offence to the indigenous gods, Buddhist deities offered an extra layer of cosmic protection.

Renewed contact with China in 600, during its short-lived Sui Dynasty (581–618), sparked fresh interest in Chinese culture. Students were sent to study there, returning with precious books and artefacts. Confucian ideas helped to inspire the rudiments of constitutional thought. A seventeen-article document, attributed to Suiko's regent Prince Shōtoku in 604 but probably appearing a little later, laid out the principles of good governance: harmony, the reward of merit and close attention to Buddhist teachings. Gluttony, flattery, sycophancy and anger, meanwhile, were strenuously to be avoided. A 'cap rank' system was introduced, so that positions at court could be awarded based on merit rather than lineage. Caps were named after six of the major Confucian values: virtue, benevolence, sincerity, propriety, justice and knowledge. Varying in colour depending on rank, they became part of a broader adoption of Chinese-style dress at the Yamato court: tunics over trousers for men; tunics over skirts for women.

Court life was enlivened, around the same time, by new musical instruments and styles of dance making their way into Yamato from China and Korea. *Gigaku*, introduced from Paekche, became especially popular: a form of dance-drama featuring brightly coloured masks representing animals or famous historical figures. Buddhist monks, nuns and temples tended to be the main conduits for these musical and dance traditions entering Yamato, as they were for Korean and Chinese medicine, astronomy and calendar-making.

Add to all this a set of 'Taika Reforms' in 646, dealing with land rights and tax and largely borrowed from Tang China, and the Yamato kingdom was beginning to look more and more like a Chinese-style state. A remarkable exception was the story that the Yamato sovereigns used the *Kojiki* and *Nihon Shoki* to tell about themselves and their place in the cosmos. The world had its beginning, it was said, in formless chaos. Heaven and Earth eventually emerged as separate realms, from lighter and denser particles of that chaos. Gods – *kami* – began to manifest, including the brother and sister deities Izanagi and Izanami.

According to the stories, one day Izanagi and Izanami are charged by the other *kami* with creating a 'drifting land'. This they do by standing on the Floating Bridge of Heaven while Izanagi stirs a spear in the formless, briny waters below. A drop of salt drips from the spear when Izanagi withdraws it, and the world's first island is created: Onogoro. Together Izanagi and Izanami descend there, are married, and Izanami gives birth to a whole host of new *kami*: the remaining islands of the archipelago, along with great seas, mountains, rivers and forests. In the *Kojiki* account, still more *kami* emerge from Izanami as she lies dying after giving birth to the fire god. From her urine, faeces and vomit emerge the *kami* of rushing water, clay and metal.

Bereft, Izanagi pursues Izanami into Yomi: the grim, sulphurous land of the dead. But so shocked is he by the sight of the maggot-ridden corpse he encounters there that he ends up leaving without her. Purifying himself in a river, new *kami* spring from his body. From his left eye comes Amaterasu, the sun goddess; from his right comes her brother Tsukuyomi, the moon god. From his nose emerges Susanoo, the trickster storm god, often depicted in art as wild and chaotic – in stark contrast to Amaterasu, who is beautiful, willowy and radiant.

Amaterasu is given the High Plain of Heaven to rule, while Tsukuyomi's domain is the night and Susanoo's the ocean. In time, Amaterasu sends her grandson, Ninigi, to rule over the islands created by Izanagi and Izanami, bestowing on him the sacred regalia: a bronze mirror, a sword and a curved jewel. Ninigi's great-grandson, Jimmu, later becomes the first human to rule the islands. He is descended not just from Amaterasu, but also from other *kami* of land and sea, allowing him to unite all of creation. From Jimmu, the *Nihon Shoki* traces a line of rulers running through to the Great Sovereigns of the sixth, seventh and early eighth centuries. No other clans are permitted divine descent in these accounts. They must make do with an adopted deity instead, who is woven into a pantheon with Amaterasu at its apex, thus mirroring the hegemony of the Yamato clan on earth.

The Great Sovereign Temmu, who reigned from 672 to 686 and probably commissioned the compilation of the *Kojiki* and *Nihon Shoki*, may have been the first of his line to refer to himself as *tennō*: 'Heavenly Sovereign', usually rendered in English as 'Emperor'. The term was then retroactively applied, all the way back to Jimmu as the first emperor. Temmu can be found opening his edicts with words that no Chinese emperor would have used: 'Hear ye the edict of an emperor who is a manifest *kami*.' While China's emperors hoped to enjoy the Mandate of Heaven, Yamato's claimed to have family up there. Such an elevated status meant that the old *Wa* name given to the people of the archipelago by the Chinese would no longer do. A Yamato envoy to China is said to have declared that henceforth his country should be known as Nihon: 'origin of the sun'. Travelling via various Asian and European languages, 'Nihon' eventually became the English word 'Japan'.

Under Emperor Temmu and then his wife Jitō, who succeeded him as *tennō* after he died, courtiers were required to be literate. That meant being able to read and understand Chinese, alongside the written versions of Japanese that were beginning to emerge. These used the Chinese script in a mixture of two ways: matching up the meaning of a Japanese word with its Chinese counterpart, or borrowing the sound of a Chinese character to represent a similar-sounding syllable in Japanese. The *Kojiki* was written in a complicated form of the meaning-borrowing method. The *Nihon Shoki* was written in Chinese, but featured songs written using the sound-borrowing method. The poems of the *Man'yōshū* were written in a combination of the two.

By the time that the *Kojiki* and *Nihon Shoki* were completed, the Yamato dynasty had a new home: Heijō-kyō, better known to posterity as Nara. Until relatively recently, the Yamato court had moved to a new location every time an emperor died: the old place became inauspicious by association, and in any case the materials – largely wood – used for palaces and shrines necessitated their regular rebuilding. Nara, by contrast, served as a capital city for more than seventy years, from 710 to 784. These decades make up a discrete period of Japanese history all by themselves, so important were they in bringing to fruition the great gathering-in of local and continental ideas that had characterised the Yamato court across the previous two centuries.

Nara was planned according to the grid-pattern layout of China's Chang'an, featuring the imperial palace in the north and two great markets in the south. Stone foundations were used for its major buildings, with strong timber frames and tiled roofs. The emperor or empress remained the supreme authority in the land, but the realm was run on a day-to-day basis by a Great Council of State (Dajōkan) whose senior posts included a chancellor alongside ministers of the right and left, each overseeing a range of specialised ministries. The minister of the left oversaw personnel alongside central, civil and popular affairs; the minister of the right meanwhile took care of war, justice, the treasury and the imperial household. By the mid-eighth century, Nara's population stood at around 100,000 people, a tenth of whom are thought to have been employed in government work.

Beyond Nara lay around sixty provinces, between them home to between 4 and 6 million people. Each was run by a governor who enjoyed sweeping powers and whose job it was to ensure that imperial taxes were paid: in rice, other goods and corvée labour – those grand new buildings in Nara were not going to build themselves. Decrees issued against vagrancy in this era reveal the pressure that people were under, from tax demands and from conscription to the imperial army: things seem often to have become so bad that families preferred to leave home and go elsewhere, including crossing the Japanese border in northern Honshū and entering what were rumoured to be wild and lawless lands.

Angry villagers seeking justice, or ambitious ones hoping for a career in the imperial bureaucracy, had to contend with the sad fact that the harmonious meritocracy dreamed of by Prince Shōtoku back in the early seventh century had failed to materialise. Control over provinces and court affairs alike depended on family and preferment. One had more chance of rising up the ranks within the Buddhist establishment, whose monks and nuns were all expected to serve the state in their own way. Emperor Temmu helped this establishment to grow, by funding the building of Buddhist temples, welcoming monks from mainland Asia, issuing restrictions on people's consumption of meat and fish and even ordering the installation of a Buddhist shrine in every household – though how many people complied, we do not know.

A number of devout emperors followed in Temmu's footsteps, including Emperor Shōmu (reigned 724–49), who responded to a smallpox outbreak that may have killed up to a quarter of the population by ordering sutra recitations at his capital and out in the provinces. Shōmu later decreed that a temple and nunnery be established in every province, for the protection of the realm and the dissemination of Buddhist teachings. When gold deposits were discovered in northern Japan, he oversaw the casting of a sixteen-metre golden statue of the cosmic Buddha Vairocana (Dainichi in Japanese). Housed in a temple in Nara called Tōdai-ji, which became for a while the centre of Buddhist learning and training in Japan, the statue required eight attempts to get right and the use of an estimated sixteen tonnes of gold along with more than twenty times that of copper. It remains in place today, within a reconstructed Tōdai-ji.

Japan's Buddhists did not always repay such kindness and largesse. Some, including a monk named Gyōki (668–749) left their monasteries to go and offer practical help to the poor. Gyōki and his disciples travelled around building bridges and roads, digging canals and establishing small monasteries, nunneries and temples offering medical care to local populations. Gyōki came to be venerated even in his own lifetime as a bodhisattva: one who postpones their own enlightenment in order to help others. He was not, however, universally appreciated. By tending to society's ills, he offered a powerful implicit criticism of the state, whose role it was to protect against such suffering in the first place.

Rather more worrying than Buddhist monks looking after other people's interests were those determined to see to their own. A monk by the name of Dōkyō, serving at Tōdai-ji in the mid-eighth century, became well known for his expertise in Buddhism's more esoteric sutras, dealing with astrology and magic, and for his powers as a healer. This drew him into the orbit of the daughter of Emperor Shōmu, who reigned as Empress Shōtoku from 764 to 770. Dōkyō and Shōtoku are rumoured to have become lovers, and Shōtoku began to give Dōkyō considerable authority in her administration. This he used to promote Buddhism, curb the power of the clans and live the high life, dressing and eating as though he himself were of royal blood.

Like many an upstart across history, Dōkyō eventually overreached himself. In 769, a rather convenient oracle was given at a shrine to the *kami* Hachiman (god of warriors), which declared that for the good of the realm Dōkyō should be made emperor. Fortunately, the empress was prompted in a dream to seek a second opinion. She dispatched a messenger to the shrine, and he returned with a new and rather less favourable oracle:

> Since the establishment of our state, the distinction
> between lord and subject has been fixed. Never has
> there been an occasion when a subject was made
> lord. The throne of Heavenly Sun succession shall be
> given to one of the imperial lineage; wicked persons
> should immediately be swept away.

Dōkyō's influence at court quickly waned, and he was eventually sent into exile. But here was a sign of the danger that Buddhism might pose to secular authorities in Japan: possessing richly resonant ideas and backed by great wealth and learning, Buddhist clergy were all too capable of reaching out directly to suffering or rebellious populations and suggesting that the time had come for a change in the country's leadership.

For the imperial family, the risks of being hoodwinked by rogue monastics was outweighed by the enduring threat of the other clans. Soon after the creation of the Dajōkan, wealthy families began to vie with one another to dominate or else subvert it, and to have their children marry into the imperial family so that one of their own might one day sit on the throne. So intense did factionalism become in Nara, and so great was the power there of the Buddhist establishment, that under Emperor Kanmu (r. 781–806) the capital was abandoned in favour of new ones: first at Nagaoka and then, from 794, at a place to be called Heian-kyō ('City of Peace and Tranquillity'), some fifty kilometres to the north of Nara.

This second site was well chosen. Mountains to the north, west and east offered natural defensive protection, the surrounding soil was rich and there was easy access via river to the Inland Sea: a body of water separating Honshū, Kyūshū and Shikoku, which had for centuries served as a vital trade and transport route. Like Nara, Heian-kyō was modelled on the Chinese city of Chang'an. The imperial palace complex was once again situated in the north of the city, its buildings constructed on stone bases with white walls, pillars of red lacquer and green glazed tiles. To the south lay two bustling city markets, east and west, home to eighty stalls between them, along with two large cherry trees, one in each market. These were there not just for aesthetic reasons: beneath the branches that bore beautiful blossoms each spring, offenders would occasionally be birched or flogged for all to see.

Some three and a half miles in length from north to south, Heian-kyō was split down the middle by a broad boulevard named Suzaku Avenue. Lined with willow trees and used for grand processions, it terminated in the south at the great Rashōmon gateway, one of eighteen around the city. Buddhist temples were, for the most part, banned from the city – the memory of their imposing presence remained raw, geographically and politically, at Nara. Japan's aristocrats, by contrast, rushed to build mansions in the most advantageous locations: typically facing on to one of the city's great avenues, and as close as possible to the imperial palace complex.

This was a city about which poetry would be written and songs sung. Known to posterity as Kyoto, it would serve as Japan's imperial capital for more than a thousand years.

# CHAPTER 3

# The Perfection of Culture

A good lover will behave as elegantly at dawn as at any other time. He drags himself out of bed with a look of dismay on his face . . . He gives a deep sigh, as if to say that the night has not been nearly long enough and that it is agony to leave.

Indeed, one's attachment to a man depends largely on the elegance of his leave-taking. When he jumps out of bed, scurries about the room, tightly fastens his trouser-sash, rolls up the sleeves of his Court cloak, over-robe, or hunting costume, stuffs his belongings into the breast of his robe and then briskly secures the outer sash – one really begins to hate him.

— Sei Shōnagon, *Pillow Book* (*Makura no Sōshi, c.* 1001)

One of the perks of being emperor or empress during the Heian period, running from 794 to 1185, was that Japan's great aristocratic families would forever be trying to catch your attention. You could expect to be plied with presents, have elegant poems written for you and be introduced to attractive sons and daughters, nieces and nephews. At its best, the imperial court at Heian-kyō was a salon, packed with sophisticated, try-hard courtiers keen to make an impression. Entertainment sometimes ran right through the night.

As lady-in-waiting to Empress Teishi, consort of Emperor Ichijō (r. 986–1011), Sei Shōnagon was at once a part of this extraordinary milieu and one of its wittiest and least forgiving critics. She poured her observations into a *Pillow Book* (*Makura no Sōshi, c.* 1001), most likely named for the fact that Sei kept the book close to her wooden pillow or perhaps in a drawer inside it. A miscellany of sorts, it is one of a number of literary innovations that marked the emergence of a definitively 'Japanese' culture out of the Chinese and Korean influences that had entered the archipelago across the preceding centuries. Where the lingua franca of much official business was Classical Chinese, the *Pillow Book* was mostly composed using *hiragana*: a new syllabic system derived from simplified Chinese characters, used for writing Japanese.

The pages of the *Pillow Book* are full of events, anecdotes, observations, pen portraits of Sei's acquaintances – and no fewer than 164 lists. Depressing Things include a dog howling in the daytime, receiving a poem that is 'old-fashioned and dull' and the sight of an exorcist who fails his client and then falls asleep. Sei's infamous distaste for the 'lower orders' comes through in her list of Unsuitable Things, which includes 'snow on the houses of common people'. Such folk, she thinks, are undeserving of these moments of fleeting beauty. It is 'especially regrettable', she adds, 'when the moonlight shines down on it'. Embarrassing Things, meanwhile, include parents who, 'convinced that their ugly child is adorable, pet him and repeat the things he has said, imitating his voice'.

For all that 'annoying', 'disagreeable' and 'hateful' things loom large in her writing, Sei Shōnagon was no mere curmudgeon. The *Pillow Book* is also a celebration of life in Heian-kyō during a period that Japanese of later centuries imagined would never be beaten for splendour and sophistication. Each season, for Sei, had its own delights, from the faint red glow of the hills at dawn on a spring day to the fireflies flitting to and fro on a summer's night. Sei found much to love, too, in the sight of baby sparrows hopping, children crawling towards some object that had captured their attention, and a lazy cat named Lady Myōbu being chased around the imperial dining room by a dog.

Through Sei's writings, we also get a vivid sense of Heian-kyō's social calendar. Cherished events included the annual Kamo Festival, held in honour of the *kami* of the Upper and Lower Kamo Shrines, who lent their protection to the city. Sei recalled witnessing the Sacred Dance of the Return, performed at the imperial palace following the festivities at the shrines:

> As the smoke rose in slender wisps from the bonfires in the garden, I listened to the clear, delicate, charmingly tremulous sound of the flute that accompanied the sacred dances. The singing also moved me greatly. Delighted by the scene, I hardly noticed that the air was piercingly cold, that my robes of beaten silk were icy, and that the hand in which I held my fan was almost frozen.

Records of events like these, in the *Pillow Book* and other aristocratic writings of the time, tended to blend recollection with an idealised sense of what *ought* to have happened. This was true especially of comments about the seasons. Why lament a humid summer's night that left you grumpy the next day when you can offer your readers a cool, breezy, fragrant one – the backdrop, perhaps, to a little romance?

Conventions had a role to play in poetry, too. An imperial

anthology called *Kokinshū* (*Collection of Poems Ancient and Modern*), compiled in 905, begins with a preface in which the court noble Ki no Tsurayuki declares that the purpose of poetry is to 'move heaven and earth, stir the feelings of gods and spirits invisible to the eye, soften the relations between men and women [and] calm the hearts of fierce warriors'. The *Kokinshū* set out to achieve these lofty aims via lyrical reflections on love, the seasons and the natural world, many of them produced in the *waka* style featuring thirty-one syllables spread across five lines in a 5-7-5-7-7 pattern:

This summer night
     About to go to bed
When the cuckoo
     Utters a single cry
     At the first light of day


Autumn has come
     And my garden is covered
In scarlet leaves,
     With no path leading through
     Since no one comes to visit

The poems of the *Kokinshū* went on to become a popular point of reference in aristocratic life, helping to set the standard for *miyabi*, or 'courtly refinement', to which men and women alike aspired. One found it in aristocratic clothing – each season had its colours and styles – and in the *shinden* design style of Heian-era homes. A lighter and more understated version of the Chinese-style Buddhist temples that had sprung up in Japan a few centuries earlier, these one-storey homes had bark-shingled roofs that curved slightly at the ends, giving a pleasing impression of weightlessness. Individual pavilions within each dwelling were connected via covered corridors, and the bare wooden floors of the entire complex were raised around a foot off the ground to ease humidity.

Heian-kyō's slightly sloping terrain allowed for canals to be dug, enlivening its main streets and channelling water into aristocratic gardens. These were often designed to represent, in miniature, some celebrated bit of landscape out in the provinces. One might find an artificial lake providing the garden's centrepiece, complete with little hills, rocks and pine trees. Relatively clement weather throughout much of the year ensured that a home's garden was frequently the focus for parties. Pillars and sliding doors allowed each pavilion to be opened up to the outdoors. Inside, curtains and bamboo blinds could be open and closed, creating space, as desired, for a large gathering or an intimate encounter.

Some of this can be seen in *Yamato-e* paintings from the Heian era. A 'blown off roof' visual technique allows viewers to peek inside aristocratic homes and see noblemen and women going about their business. Emotions can be difficult to read, since people were typically represented using a minimalist technique whose name speaks for itself: *hikime kagihana* translates as 'a line for the eye, a hook for the nose'. Still, there is plenty to appreciate, from lavish clothing and the decorated screens behind which women of high birth might sit, to outdoor scenes featuring women sitting on their verandas and admiring immaculately kept gardens and blossoming cherry trees.

\*

Over the course of the Heian era, the locus of power shifted steadily away from the imperial palace complex and towards the grand homes of the nobility. The city's founder Emperor Kanmu and his successors had been strong enough leaders to keep Buddhist clergy and feuding families alike largely in check. Kanmu was particularly keen to clamp down on corruption within the country's Buddhist establishment. He introduced measures against Buddhist temples lending money at exorbitant interest rates and against clergy fathering children or claiming to work miracles. Only people of good character and sound learning would henceforth be considered for the life of a monk or nun.

And yet at the heart of Japanese politics lay a critical weakness. The Yamato family had always presented themselves as first among equals, performing the acts of diplomacy required to persuade the other great families to go along with their vision. Even after they began to claim divine descent, no real taboo existed against challenging their power as long as appearances were preserved. Across the ninth century, the northern branch of the Fujiwara family did precisely this, enjoying an unprecedented rise to influence at court. They married into the imperial family, supplied regents for young and impressionable emperors (encouraging their abdication when they became less pliant), took over key administrative posts and steadily turned swathes of the countryside from imperial land into their private estates.

The person most closely associated with this important shift in Japanese politics was Fujiwara no Michinaga (966–1028). He was the supreme political operator of his day; a man who loved luxury, power, drink and women and who seems to have inspired, in those who knew him, awe rather than great affection. His proudest boast was that he had managed to marry four of his daughters to emperors. Japanese of later centuries would add to this his encouragement of one of Japan's greatest literary names: Murasaki Shikibu, author of *The Tale of Genji*.

Born around 973, Murasaki had married in her mid-twenties but lost her husband two or three years later, in 1001. She feared that life would pass her by until, it seems, early chapters of what became *The Tale of Genji* began to circulate at court: the story of a handsome, sensitive, accomplished and irrepressibly amorous prince called Genji, and his descendants. These chapters came to the attention of Michinaga, who supplied Murasaki's scribes with high-quality brushes, ink and paper and then chose her as a lady-in-waiting to his daughter Shōshi when she became a consort to Emperor Ichijō. Michinaga even seems to have tried his luck with Murasaki, writing her the occasional piece of suggestive verse but receiving only a polite rebuff.

Murasaki Shikibu's diary, together with *The Tale of Genji*, Sei Shōnagon's *Pillow Book* and a variety of other writings, including *The Tales of Ise (Ise Monogatari)*, together give us a window into court life at a point in history that many Japanese came to regard as the perfection of culture. Alongside poetry, gifts and a bit of witty repartee went leisure pursuits including hunting, excursions on horseback, backgammon, archery, competitions to discern different sorts of tea and incense and a game called *kemari*, which bore a passing resemblance to football.

At the same time, the requirements of status – gaining it,

displaying it, holding on to it – could be onerous. As a child, an aspiring courtier would have to copy out poems in Classical Chinese, as a means both of learning the language and of acquiring skills in calligraphy that might demonstrate their sophistication. Later, men and women alike would need to understand precisely which fabrics, colours and motifs were appropriate to wear given one's social status. Purple, for example, was associated with the court's highest elites. Artfully combining the colours available to you was a mark of your sophistication. When Murasaki Shikibu, in her diary, describes at length what people wear at court, she is not being tedious or seeking to pad her account: she is noting the powers of aesthetic judgement of all those around her – congratulating a given courtier on combining, for example, a robe of grape-coloured brocade with a jacket of green and cherry. A talent for poetry was of course indispensable, too. One needed to be able to conjure fresh verses on the spot, to match the mood of a moment, and to commit more considered lines to paper as part of a courtship. Woe betide the person who failed to strike the right note, or whose handwriting appeared careless.

Personal grooming, too, required much time and energy, particularly for women. White skin and glowing cheeks were highly prized, and required the application of powder and rouge. Teeth were dyed black and eyebrows plucked. All this was designed largely with the aim of attracting men in mind, leading to the kind of nocturnal visit that Sei Shōnagon describes in the *Pillow Book* – sometimes comprising an affair, sometimes as part of a highly choreographed courtship ritual intended to culminate in marriage. And yet most of an aristocratic woman's time would be spent in her home, alone or with female companions. The ability under the law to inherit and keep property gave women an important degree of security, especially in a society where a man might have a number of wives but a woman only one husband. But even someone living as privileged a life as Sei Shōnagon seems to have felt the emptiness of this existence now and again, noting as she does in her lists the disappointments of an undelivered letter, an inadequate reply and a visitor who turns out not to be the person for whom she had been waiting.

Alongside all these pressures and potential disappointments ran the problem of uncertainty. Court life was underwritten by income from private estates called *shō*, which were owned by aristocratic families and benefited from grants of exemption from government tax – a big contributor to the steady decline of imperial authority in Heian-kyō was the loss of taxable land to private interests. When crops failed, famine became a real threat. This was true even in a city like Heian-kyō, where it ranked alongside disease outbreaks, petty crime and the rapid spread of fire as serious threats to all that the likes of Sei Shōnagon and Murasaki Shikibu held dear.

In difficult times, courtiers of the Heian era often turned, for solace or in an attempt at understanding, to a couple of relatively new schools of Buddhism: Tendai and Shingon. Both had roots in China. Tendai had been established by a monk named Saichō (767–822), who set himself up on Mount Hiei, overlooking Heian-kyō. Where some schools of Buddhism taught that the path to enlightenment required great austerity, perhaps across many lifetimes, Saichō taught what he called 'Buddhahood for all': the Buddha nature resided within everyone, here and now. One had only to nourish it in everyday life and via a range of contemplative practices. The sect's main scripture, the *Lotus Sutra*, was regarded as the Buddha's final sermon, in which he revealed that Buddhahood was attainable not just by the few but by all.

Shingon, founded by another monk, Kūkai (774–835), taught that all of reality is a manifestation of Dainichi. Happily for advocates of Shingon, the characters for Dainichi mean 'great' and 'sun', making it easy for expedient connections to be made with the imperial family's divine ancestor the sun goddess Amaterasu. Based on Mount Kōya, Shingon made heavy use in its rituals of mandalas, mantras and gestures known as mudras. It was more esoteric than Tendai, with its most important teachings communicated only in secret, between masters and suitably prepared disciples. The latter included aristocrats with enough time on their hands to learn the required practices: Shingon's exclusivity was part of its attraction for those living at the apex of a hierarchical society.

For all their differences, Tendai and Shingon were both part of the broad Mahayana ('Great Vehicle') tradition of Buddhism. This had coalesced in India around the time that Himiko had lived, and spread from there into China, Korea, Japan and elsewhere. It was characterised by a belief in salvation for all and in a cosmos that is home to many different buddhas and bodhisattvas, enabling it to coexist alongside and draw from other traditions including Taoism and Shintō. In Japan, Mahayana Buddhism became influential in the arts thanks to its teachings about the illusory nature of reality, the evanescence of life and the workings of karma.

In diaries and miscellanies from the Heian era, religion appears as a matter both of social convention and of real fear and longing. At one point in the *Pillow Book*, Sei pictures a group of aristocrats on retreat at a temple, all rushing down a corridor 'to be the first before the Buddha' in the temple's main room. Elsewhere she writes, only slightly tongue in cheek, that a preacher ought ideally to be easy on the eye. At the same time, we find people going to great lengths to understand, influence or escape from various gods and spirits, alongside goblins, demons, foxes showing malevolent intent and all manner of ghosts, including one who was believed to haunt Heian-kyō's Rashōmon gateway. Attention was paid to discerning omens and determining auspicious versus inauspicious timings for this or that undertaking, from cutting one's hair to waging a war. Dreams were thought to contain predictions of the future, and some believed that they could see fire leaving a person's body just a few hours or days before they died.

The Chinese principles of *yin* and *yang* underlay a great deal of this, as they did the medical ideas and treatments of the time, including choices of herbal remedies. Other ailments were thought to be caused by evil spirits, some belonging to people who had been wronged in life and now sought revenge from beyond the grave. Exorcists like the one whose failure and subsequent slumber Sei Shōnagon included on her list of Depressing Things were supposed to use magical incantations to transfer an evil spirit from their client into their assistant, often a young woman, at which point the spirit would identify itself and the exorcist could banish it entirely.

\*

One of the useful things about Buddhism, from the point of view of the Heian era's political operators, was its ideal of renouncing the world at some point in one's life. A person could make a pious show of taking Buddhist vows, as a sign of leaving public life, only to then begin pulling strings from behind the scenes. The pioneer of this approach, which came to be known as *insei* ('cloistered rule'), was Emperor Go-Sanjō, who retired to a Buddhist monastery in 1073. His son and successor Emperor Shirakawa used the system particularly well, retiring while still in his thirties and spending the following four decades working against his enemies from behind the scenes – in everything from who was appointed to important administrative posts to the state of the imperial family finances.

Cloistered rule helped to temper the political influence of the Fujiwara clan. Its obvious downside, however, was that it represented a further fragmenting of power in Japan, taking the country away from the imperial state model that had worked so well under the likes of Emperor Kanmu in the eighth century. The Tendai and Shingon sects contributed to this process, growing wealthy from land holdings and employing warrior monks to intimidate religious and secular enemies alike – to the point, now and again, of burning down rival monasteries.

While all this was going on in and around Heian-kyō, change was afoot in the lands beyond. Officials sent out to the provinces as governors or estate managers had begun to build up their own manorial holdings, putting together private armies to secure them and then passing them on to their children. One of the most important of these rising provincial families was the Taira. Back in the early ninth century, a thinning of the imperial family's considerable – and costly – ranks had taken place, in which a number of collateral branches were given new surnames and sent out into the countryside to find their fortunes. A grandson of Emperor Kanmu named Prince Takamune had been given the surname Taira, and his descendants had settled on the Chiba peninsula, near present-day Tokyo. Rivalling the Taira in their reputation as warriors was the Minamoto clan, likewise of imperial stock. Some of this clan's members were employed by the Fujiwara to keep rivals and criminals in line both within Heian-kyō and beyond.

Provincial Japan was far from being the dull and inconsequential place of aristocratic imaginings. One was less likely to find there the courtly tendency to idealise nature: to work the land was to recognise flora and fauna alike as wild, hostile and in need of taming – with axe, spear or bow and arrow. Nor was there as much patience for whimsical pastimes like tea-tasting or giggling at some slightly amusing breach of etiquette (the word for something funny in this sense was *okashi*, and it survives to this day in the Japanese language). But rural life was not all toil and misery. There were *saibara* (folk songs) and *dengaku* (field dances accompanied by flutes and drums). Buddhist monks and nuns wandered the countryside telling stories, singing songs and dancing as a means of conveying to people without any education the key claims – and forfeits – of Buddhist tradition. Travelling entertainers offered juggling, puppetry and comic mime satirising the country's aristocratic and Buddhist elites, plying their trade both in the provinces and on the streets of the capital.

From the tenth century onwards, warriors increasingly

found work in Heian-kyō, employed as bodyguards by nobles who feared either that inter-familial feuding might turn violent or that some of the capital's criminals might catch up with them. At least one noble was known to take off his finery and valuables and conceal them in the floor of his carriage when he travelled. His plan, should he be waylaid, was to protest that he had already been robbed. Service of this kind, from which the word 'samurai' derives (*saburau* means 'to serve'), tended to be rendered by men who hoped that their martial skills might gain them the kind of access to preferment that hitherto had required a privileged birth and rigorous training in poetry and calligraphy.

The dangers of militarising court politics became clear in the 1150s, when a dispute over the imperial succession turned violent. One side employed Taira warriors to press their case, the other signed up some Minamoto, and two battles were fought within the confines of the capital: the Hōgen Incident (1156) and the Heiji Incident (1159). Homes were burned down, innocent bystanders were killed and enemies' heads were removed and placed on public display. It was all about as far from the society conjured by Sei Shōnagon and Murasaki Shikibu as one could imagine. But it was a taste of the world to come.

# CHAPTER 4

# The World of the Warlord

Long before the first severed heads appeared in Heian-kyō, there was a sense among the city's inhabitants that their treasured existence might be coming to an end. In 985, a Tendai monk by the name of Genshin wrote a book, inspired by teachings imported from China, called *Anthology on Rebirth in the Pure Land* (*Ōjō Yōshū*). In it, he laid out the conventional three-part division of time in Buddhist thought: the first flourishing of Buddhist ideas and practices, their steady decline thereafter and finally the age of the 'Latter-Day of the Law' (*mappō*), in which the practices required for a person's salvation become all but impossible to perform.

Genshin's book helped to popularise the idea that the world was about to enter this final stage, and that people should look for help to one of Mahayana Buddhism's most important figures: the celestial Buddha, Amida. He was said to have vowed that anyone who called faithfully on his name by reciting the *nembutsu* – 'I take refuge in Amida Buddha' – would be reborn, after death, in his Pure Land. There, he or she would find the perfect conditions for working towards freedom from the cycle of death and rebirth. The popularity of Genshin's book was no doubt helped along by the trailer he provided for the afterlife:

Looking at his own body, it becomes purplish gold in
colour. He is gowned naturally in jewelled garments.
Rings, bracelets, a crown of jewels and other ornaments in
countless profusion adorn his body . . . Flocks of wild ducks,
geese and mandarin ducks fly about in the distance and near
at hand. One may see multitudes from all the worlds being
born into this land like sudden showers of rain.

One of the first prominent noblemen to invest in this idea
was the great patriarch Fujiwara no Michinaga, who had an
Amida Hall built as part of the Hōjō-ji temple complex to
which he retired when he took Buddhist vows. He died, in
1027, surrounded by statues of Amida along with *raigō* paintings. These depicted Amida's arrival on earth, often attended
by bodhisattvas, to whisk someone away to his Pure Land.

The chaos that engulfed Japan's capital in the 1150s must
have added credence to the idea that this was the end of days.
From the clash of Minamoto with Taira forces during the Heiji
Incident of 1159, a general named Taira no Kiyomori emerged
victorious. He proved as impressive a political operator as Fujiwara no Michinaga had once been. Kiyomori installed one of
his daughters as consort to Emperor Takakura, took over some
of the major offices of state, lived the high life at his Rokuhara
mansion and dealt brutally with his enemies.

All this became too much for an imperial prince named
Mochihito, who was deprived by Kiyomori first of some
land and later of the opportunity to succeed his father as
emperor – Kiyomori moved swiftly to sew up the succession
for his own grandson instead. A little whispering in Mochihito's ear from a member of the Minamoto clan seems to

have been all it took for him to produce, in 1180, a stinging public rebuke of Kiyomori's behaviour. Mochihito accused Kiyomori of rebellion, theft, corruption, killing and general mistreatment of everyone from the emperor downwards. Invoking the authority of revered historical figures including Prince Shōtoku and Emperor Temmu, Mochihito called on people to topple the upstart Kiyomori.

Taira forces quickly tracked down and murdered Prince Mochihito, but the rebellion was not over. Minamoto no Yoritomo, whose father Kiyomori had defeated during the Heiji Incident, managed to gather together allies in eastern Japan and wage war against the Taira from his base in the coastal village of Kamakura. The conflict came to be known as the Genpei War, after the Chinese readings of the characters for Minamoto (*gen*) and Taira (*hei/pei*). In fact, it was more a protracted series of battles than an all-out war. But it was momentous nonetheless. By the time hostilities ceased, five years later in 1185, Taira no Kiyomori was dead and Minamoto no Yoritomo had gained effective control of large swathes of the country.

Kamakura now displaced Heian-kyō as the political and administrative centre of Japan. Seeking to maintain the fiction of imperial supremacy – as many an ambitious leader of the country would across centuries to come – Yoritomo had himself appointed Sei-i-Taishōgun by the emperor in 1192. The title meant 'Commander-in-Chief of the Expeditionary Forces against the Barbarians', and in keeping with this sense of a temporary military operation, Yoritomo's administration became known as a *bakufu*, or 'tent government'. Warrior-constables were sent out to maintain law and order in each province, while estate managers oversaw the running of private estates, receiving in exchange a percentage of their produce.

Many a noble in Heian-kyō – or 'Kyoto', as it is often referred to in this and subsequent eras – must have found the award of the title of Sei-i-Taishōgun, sometimes shortened to simply shōgun, rather ironic. Far from being a crusher of barbarians, Yoritomo was himself, for all his ancient links to the imperial family, if not barbarous than at least a little rustic and uncouth. One had only to compare the literature of this new age with what had gone before for this to become painfully clear. The *Pillow Book* and *The Tale of Genji* suggested a calm and gentle court culture given to poetry and romance, play and display. By contrast, *The Tale of the Heike* (*Heike monogatari*) rejoiced in grisly episodes from the Genpei War: people are forever being stabbed, cut, decapitated, drowned or impaled.

This did not mean that the world of Murasaki Shikibu now vanished entirely. Rather, it changed. Space was made for martial virtues: where the imperial armies of old, stuffed with reluctant conscripts, had rarely achieved feats about which songs would be sung, personal bravery on the battlefield now came to be highly valued. At the same time, although the imperial state had shown itself painfully vulnerable to fracture and capture – Japan's emperors remained relatively powerless during the era of the Kamakura *bakufu* (1192–1333) – the ideal of *miyabi*, 'courtly refinement', proved surprisingly robust. Far from dismissing as useless or effeminate the arts associated with the imperial court, Japan's new warrior elite regarded proficiency in them as a mark of their new, elevated status.

Even *The Tale of the Heike*, for all its gory episodes, was deeply poetic in its telling of how the great Taira clan and its tyrannical leader Kiyomori met their end. One of the most influential passages on later Japanese culture told of a meeting between a Minamoto warrior by the name of Kumagai no Naozane and a mysterious young Taira rival. By this point in the tale, the Taira are all but finished and many are seeking to escape the battlefield aboard ships. Kumagai however still wishes to do battle with a worthy adversary:

> He rode towards the shore and found a warrior there
> wearing a silk hitatare [formal linen robe] embroidered
> with cranes under delicately tinted green armour, a helmet
> with spreading horns, a sword with gold fittings and, on
> his back, arrows fletched with mottled feathers. He carried
> a lacquered, rattan-wrapped bow and rode a dappled grey
> with a gold-trimmed saddle.

In the expected warrior way of the time, Kumagai calls out a challenge before riding over to the man. The two fall to the ground from their horses and Kumagai rips off his enemy's helmet to find a handsome young boy, his face lightly powdered and his teeth blackened. Kumagai wrestles with his conscience – he doesn't want to kill him:

> 'What I want, you know, is to spare you,
> but the great host of men on my side
> will never allow you to get away.
> Rather than leave your fate to others,
> I prefer to see to it myself
> and to pray for you in the afterlife.'

Tears in his eyes, Kumagai kills the young boy and removes his head. He goes to take off the boy's robe, planning to wrap his head in it and present it as a trophy to his commander Minamoto no Yoshitsune, a half-brother of Yoritomo and one of the most celebrated warriors in Japanese history. As he does so, he finds around the boy's waist a brocade bag containing a flute. The boy was not just beautiful, he had a soul, too – who on his own side, Kumagai reflects, would have brought a musical instrument into battle?

When Kumagai presents the head to Yoshitsune and his entourage, everyone in attendance begins to cry. Kumagai later learns the boy's name: Atsumori. The episode ends with Kumagai stricken by grief and determined to retire to the life of a monk:

> It is a touching thought indeed
> that the giddy charms of music
> served to turn a warrior's mind
> to praise the way traced by the Buddha.

The key to Minamoto no Yoritomo's success in establishing a brand-new form of government in Japan was his ability to win allies to his cause by parcelling out valuable tracts of land which were, strictly speaking, not his to give – they belonged ultimately to the emperor. Coalitions of the self-interested rarely last long, and after Yoritomo's untimely death in 1199, following a fall from his horse, the Kamakura *bakufu* threatened to unravel. Yoritomo's widow, Masako, was instrumental in preventing that from happening. She kept the couple's sons in line, and when the last of those sons died in 1219, leaving no direct descendants to carry on the shogunal line, she and other members of her natal family, the Hōjō, took over. They developed a practice of selecting young, pliable candidates for shōgun from among the ranks of the Fujiwara and imperial families, while retaining control themselves as regents.

The old imperial state had meanwhile not entirely gone away. Some parts of the country remained under its control, and when it came to foreign policy the *bakufu* felt the need to consult the court. So it was that when, in 1268, envoys arrived from Kublai Khan requesting friendly relations between Japan and the Mongolian Empire – while threatening 'resort to arms' should they be refused – the *bakufu* and the imperial court considered the matter together. They decided simply to ignore both this request and several others that followed in its wake.

By 1274, Kublai Khan had had enough of waiting. He made good on his threat, sending forces first to the islands of Tsushima and Iki, located between the southern Korean peninsula and Kyūshū, and then to Hakata Bay in Kyūshū itself. The *bakufu* was prepared for an invasion, but not for the weapons and tactics used by the invaders. For all that courtiers might have regarded their warrior rivals as rather boorish, samurai life and warfare possessed – ideally, at least – elements of honour and artistry. A warrior's code of sorts, compiled in the mid-thirteenth century by a member of the Hōjō family for his son, states that a warrior should believe in the gods and the buddhas and be mindful of the workings of karma, not just in his own life but in the lives of the generations to come. He must be skilled in the martial arts and treat duty (*giri*) with the utmost seriousness.

The samurai spoke of their calling as the 'Way of the Horse

and Bow', and at the beginning of a battle a special whis-
tling arrow would be fired into the air by a samurai on horseback in order to alert the *kami* to the valorous deeds that
were about to be done. He would then pick a single, suitably
worthy target, call out to them, and seek to dispatch them
with an arrow. When the fighting was over, care would be
taken to record the outcome: for the honour of that samurai
and his house, and for the reward that he might then expect
for his loyalty and valour. As ever in a mountainous country
where agricultural land was at a premium, this would hope-
fully take the form of an expansion of the samurai's holdings.
Evidence would of course be required, often taking the form
of the severed head of the defeated opponent.

Even allowing for the fact that only an exceptionally dim-
witted warrior would have expected his Mongolian enemies
to observe such niceties (or indeed speak Japanese), the
samurai defending Kyūshū were no doubt shocked by what
they encountered: deafening gongs and drums used by the
advancing troops, great thickets of poison-tipped arrows
arcing towards their positions and exploding bombs capable
of inspiring panic in samurai and steed alike. The samurai,
though, were not without advantages of their own. We know
from painted scrolls from this era, together with a number of
surviving examples, that their armour was of the strong, boxy
*yoroi* sort, formed from scales of lacquered iron and leather
tied together with cords and worn over a robe and trousers.
Helmets, too, were made from iron, worn over a soft cap and
with a neck guard formed from tied scales. This armour was
lighter than European equivalents, because horses in Japan
were generally less muscular than those used in Europe and

if a rider desired speed and agility on the battlefield then he could not afford to over-tax his mount.

Samurai carried no shields, but in some cases they bene-fited from those used by foot soldiers fighting alongside them. Most important of all, they enjoyed the protection of the gods. How else to explain the fact that soon after the Mongol forces returned to their boats – a temporary tactical withdrawal, perhaps, or else the end of an expedition whose task was simply to probe the enemy's defences – great storms were said to have blown up and destroyed many of those vessels? As many as 13,500 soldiers, or around one-third of the total invasion force, are thought never to have made it home.

Whatever the combination involved of samurai skill, divine favour and freak weather conditions, the first Mongol invasion of Japan was a failure. The Great Khan persisted nonetheless, and sent fresh envoys. The *bakufu* had them be-headed and continued to prepare for a new invasion. It came in 1281, and consisted of perhaps three times the number of troops sent before, divided into 'eastern route' and 'southern route' armies. The eastern army attacked via Tsushima and Iki once again, while the southern army sailed from southern China to Iki. For reasons that are unclear, the eastern army left Tsushima and Iki for Kyūshū without waiting for their comrades. They also opted to attack positions including Hakata Bay which they must have known would have been fortified in the years since the first invasion.

The result was a disaster for the Mongols. Volleys of arrows were fired at the eastern army as they advanced, while out at sea their ships were approached by small boats with samurai aboard – bearing peace terms, or so the Mongols appear to have assumed. They only realised their mistake when the boats suddenly let down their masts and used them as bridges to board the much larger Mongol vessels. Some samurai, desperate perhaps to get ahead of their comrades and make a name for themselves, swam out to the Mongol ships in full armour. Close combat followed, during which the quality of the Japanese swords and swordsmanship became decisive. The Mongols meanwhile compounded their mistakes by bringing their ships together for defence, using chains and planks. When powerful winds began to blow up around them, the damage and loss of life was much worse than it might otherwise have been.

The story of 'divine winds' (*kami-kaze*) helping to save Japan back in 1274 is disputed. But it is clear in the records kept by both sides that in 1281 the weather really did play a role in bringing the Mongol invasion to an end. For the Japanese, it was divine intervention: an answer to the many prayers being said around the country. For the Mongols, it was more like black magic. Witnesses claimed to have seen a great serpent thrashing around in the waters, and to have smelled sulphur on the air.

The Kamakura shogunate, under its Hōjō regency, survived for another half-century after the failed Mongol invasions. It was finally felled not by a cataclysmic battle but by a poor hiring decision. Emperor Go-Daigo was exiled to the Oki Islands in 1331 after seeking to restore himself to power. He escaped, and a *bakufu* army was sent against him and his allies. A general by the name of Ashikaga Takauji was chosen to lead that army, but in 1333 he defected to Emperor Go-Daigo and helped him to destroy the Kamakura *bakufu* and restore imperial power. Three years later, Takauji turned on the emperor, who fled south to the picturesque Yoshi-no mountains near Nara while Takauji created a new *bakufu* in Kyoto. For sixty years, power in Japan was split between a southern court under Emperor Go-Daigo and a northern court under a new imperial line installed by Takauji as his puppets. At last, under Takauji's grandson, Yoshimitsu, peace was agreed and the northern court won out.

The Ashikaga *bakufu* lasted, in one form or another, from 1336 through to 1573. The era is often referred to as the Muromachi period, after the neighbourhood in Kyoto where the new *bakufu* was headquartered. The latter part of the period is one of the most blood-soaked in Japanese history, but its early decades were marked by the successful combining of courtly and warrior cultures. In the process, the sights and sounds of rural Japan made their presence felt in the country's capital: plays, comic sketches, the chanting and singing of itinerant Buddhists and storytellers, and the often melancholy use of nature imagery that gives the work of great poets like Saigyō (1118–90) its force:

> In a tree standing
> Beside a desolate field,
> The voice of a dove
> Calling to its companions –
> Lonely, terrible evening.

> Should I blame the moon
> For bringing forth this sadness?
> As if it pictured grief?
> Lifting up my troubled face,
> I regard it through my tears.

Where Heian-era courtiers had thought relatively little of the countryside, having most of what they needed – rural recreation and temple retreats included – within a short distance of the capital, from the late 1100s onwards we find poets and painters much more willing to travel and explore. Saigyō was perhaps the first great poet to work in this way: a warrior-turned-Buddhist-priest who was steeped in the idea of *mappō*, the Buddhist end-times. Travel was bound up with a sense of impermanence (*aware*) and of loneliness (*sabi*): two key themes in Japanese aesthetics, which have roots in this era. To these we might add 'resonance' (*yojō*): the potential for very few words to carry a rich variety of meanings, if the poet is skilled enough and their hearer or reader suitably prepared.

As the political power of Japan's aristocracy waned, so the great Buddhist sects with which their fortunes had long been intertwined, Tendai and Shingon, faced challenges of their own. One strand, in what is sometimes regarded as Japanese Buddhism's Reformation, was represented by new Pure Land schools founded by Hōnen (1133–1212) and Shinran (1173–1262). Both men trained at the Tendai headquarters on Mount Hiei, where they came into contact with the Pure Land teachings. Hōnen went on to preach what came to be known as the 'exclusive *nembutsu*': all one needed in order to be saved was sincerely to seek refuge in Amida Buddha by reciting the *nembutsu* – no other practices were required, no rank and no riches. Shinran later left Hiei, too, and for a while became a disciple of Hōnen. A crackdown on the exclusive *nembutsu* teaching, after lobbying by rival Buddhist sects and rumours that Hōnen's followers were using it as a licence to do whatever they pleased (on the basis that Amida would rescue them regardless), led to the exile and separation of Hōnen and Shinran. They continued to teach, however, and in time Hōnen's followers formed the Pure Land School while Shinran's formed the True Pure Land School.

For Shinran, human beings in the present age were so weak that not only could they not achieve salvation by themselves, they could not even ask for it. A person was inspired or willed by Amida to recite the *nembutsu*. Alongside this radical rejection of 'self-power' (*jiriki*) in favour of 'other-power' (*tariki*), Shinran helped to pioneer the idea of married priests and lay communities. He married and raised a family of his own in Echigo province, in north central Honshū, gathering around him a rural following consisting of lower-ranking warriors, farmers, artisans and merchants. Shinran taught them that conventional morality would only take them so far. They ought to reflect, as deeply and honestly as they could, on their real failings. This, it was to be hoped, would lead to a profound sense of their own inadequacy, opening them up to Amida's saving intervention.

As the True Pure Land sect (*Jōdo Shinshū*) developed, congregations formed and began to meet around once per month to recite the *nembutsu* together, at first in one another's homes and later in purpose-built *dōjō*. At the grassroots level, this encouraged a great deal more independence among the laity than in other Buddhist sects. At the top, Shinran's descendants became the leaders, or 'patriarchs', of the sect. Their ability to sway their followers on matters both religious and political was set to become a thorn in the side of Japan's warrior elite.

Two other important strands emerged in Buddhism during this period. The first was Zen, whose teachings are traditionally credited to a sixth-century Indian monk named Bodhidharma. He is said to have travelled to China, offered teachings to Emperor Wu, the cryptic nature of which the latter found utterly mystifying, and then later to have meditated for nine years in front of a wall until his legs grew weak and fell off. Somewhere amid all this legendary detail is a man who brought to China a set of teachings, rooted in Mahayana Buddhism, which were heavily focused on meditation and on the dispelling of the fantasies and illusions that keep a person from experiencing reality as it is.

Bodhidharma is remembered in China as the first patriarch of the Chan sect of Buddhism, on which Taoism is thought to have been a significant influence during its development. Chan teachings were brought to Japan by two monks who trained in the Tendai sect and later travelled to Song China. Eisai (1141–1215) brought back teachings on meditation and the use of *kōan*: riddles designed to reveal the inadequacy of words and concepts. These formed the basis for the Rinzai Zen branch of Japanese Buddhism. Dōgen (1200–1253) returned from China with teachings that focused more on meditation alone. His branch of Buddhism became known as Sōtō Zen.

Where the teachings of Hōnen, Shinran, Eisai and Dōgen all had roots in Chinese Buddhism, the final strand to emerge in this era was firmly, even aggressively Japanese. Nichiren (1222–1282) was yet another refugee from Tendai. He took as his starting point the idea of *mappō* and a fear of what appeared to be Japan's imminent collapse – for which he blamed, in no small part, the country's Buddhist sects. This was no idle slander: in the course of his spiritual quest, Nichiren had tried Pure Land, Zen, Shingon and Tendai teachings for himself. He found them all wanting.

Nichiren concluded that salvation, both individual and collective, was to be found only in the *Lotus Sutra*. Such was this sutra's power, thought Nichiren, that a person need not actually understand it. They need only express their faith in it, saying or chanting: 'I devote myself to the Wonderful Law of the *Lotus Sutra*.' Failure to do so, Nichiren prophesied in 1260, would result in the invasion of Japan by a foreign power. The arrival of the first Mongol envoys in 1268 seemed, to Nichiren, to be the fulfilment of his prophecy, and he urged the authorities to take him seriously. They did not, briefly exiling him instead. But Nichiren's forceful character, his love of Japan, and the practical advice that he offered for everyday living helped ensure the continuation after his death of a major Buddhist sect bearing his name.

Japan's new Buddhist sects together had a profound effect on Japanese life and arts. Zen in particular became essential to the world of the warrior. Where Pure Land Buddhism insisted on human weakness and the need to rely upon Amida Buddha, Zen focused on self-power (*jiriki*): disciplined practices via which one might work out one's own enlightenment. As an ethic, this appealed to samurai of the Kamakura and Muromachi periods. As a mode of creating and appreciating art, wordless and intuitive, Zen proved to be extraordinarily fertile.

In Song China, Chan priests often doubled as painters, composers of poetry and connoisseurs of all kinds of crafts.

That soon became true of Japan, too, where among the most celebrated of the painter-priests was Sesshū Tōyō (1420–1506). He painted in a Chinese monochrome ink style known in Japanese as *sumi-e*, most likely learning the rudiments of his craft at the local Zen temple to which he was sent at the age of ten. He later moved to Kyoto, living and studying for twenty years at Shōkoku temple, right next door to the palace of the Ashikaga shoguns.

An important element of Sesshū's training would have been to study works by Chinese masters. Many of these were landscapes, painted not as this or that particular mountain or waterfall appeared in real life but rather via a set of stylised ideals: for how a forest partially obscured by mist ought to look, or how a waterfall ought to throw spray into the air. Human figures, if there were any, would usually be tiny and indistinct, emphasising the sheer immensity of the natural world around them.

Sesshū revered the Song-era masters and was inspired by what he saw of China's magnificent landscape when he made a brief visit in 1468–9. Returning to Japan at the height of his powers, he produced celebrated works including *View of Ama-no-Hashidate*. However, Sesshū depicted this scenic bay, located on Honshū's west coast around 40 miles north of Kyoto, not via the sort of stylised images favoured in China but instead as he saw them: misty mountains in the background and in the foreground the bay's famous pine-covered sandbar.

Zen made its presence felt in other medieval and early modern arts besides, many of which would one day be considered quintessentially 'Japanese'. In the Heian era, landscape gardening for private homes had borrowed the Chinese ideal of representing the natural world in miniature: notable lakes, rivers, forests and mountains were reproduced as ponds (some large enough to go boating on), streams, pine-topped artificial islands and carefully crafted arrangements of rocks. Under the influence of Pure Land Buddhism, some nobles had 'paradise gardens' created for themselves, in which un-usual plants and animals helped conjure the strange beauty of the next life. Under the influence of Zen, landscaping became more abstract. The *karesansui* ('dry mountain water') style, designed to be viewed as an aid to contemplation rather than walked on, featured relatively little greenery and instead used rocks and raked sand or gravel to represent water. The garden at Ryōanji temple in Kyoto features fifteen stones set amid raked white sand, in such a way that from any given angle only fourteen will be visible. One stone will always obscure another. Why? Some say that the stones represent islands of consciousness within a larger emptiness, with no single point of consciousness – including that of the viewer – capable of apprehending reality in its fullness.

The tea ceremony, too, claimed strong links to Zen. The practice of drinking tea had reached Japan along with Bud-dhism back in the sixth century. It had since largely died out, only to be reintroduced by Eisai. One of tea's great benefits, he thought, was that it helped monks to stay awake during meditation. It gained additional value in later years as an increasingly formalised means of welcoming guests, taking place not in the lavish settings favoured in China but rather in simple, rustic surrounds: a thatched tea-room, with earth-en walls. Japan's great tea master, Sen no Rikyū (1522–1591), contributed the radical idea that all are equal in the tea-room. Having first washed their hands in an act of symbolic cleansing, guests would proceed along a garden path and then enter the tea-room humbly on their knees, leaving their swords – and with them, their status – outside. Rikyū also helped to give the tea ceremony its *wabi-sabi* aesthetic: withered, imperfect and carrying a sense of spiritual longing. Asked on one occasion whether the garden was clean enough, Rikyū shook a nearby tree to give it the perfect scattering of leaves.

Within the performing arts, one of the great developments of the Muromachi period was Nō theatre. Its plays were inspired by the poetry and great tales of the past, and were performed on sparsely furnished cypress-wood stages. The main actor wore a mask, finely crafted so that the play of light across it would combine with the actor's slow, deliberate movements and gestures to convey a range of subtle emotions. A second actor played a more minor, unmasked role, while off to one side of the stage sat a small group of musicians and singers heightening the drama with flutes, drums, chants and cries.

Like Zen gardens and the tea ceremony, Nō was both contemplative and rewarding of connoisseurship. Its great pioneer was the playwright Zeami (1363–1443), who flourished under the patronage of the shogun Yoshimitsu, celebrated among other achievements for building Kyoto's Golden Pavilion (Kinkaku-ji). Zeami wanted Nō to be for everyone, but to get the most out of its plays one needed to be well-versed in the storylines and characters – and thus able to appreciate this most minimalist and abstract of performing arts. The difficulty of Nō was enhanced by Zeami's requirement for his actors to master *monomane*: 'imitating things' not by mimicking their outward appearances but by finding and expressing their essence.

Did all these medieval innovations in religion and the arts mean that the samurai were going soft? Not a bit of it. The Ashikaga *bakufu* was no less vulnerable to ambitious outsiders than the Kamakura *bakufu* before it. The difference this time, as the Ashikaga shoguns watched power begin to slip through their fingers, was that one *bakufu* would not be replaced by another. Order was about to give way to a war of all against all.

# CHAPTER 5

# The Dream of Unity

For the people of Kyoto, the downside to residing in the imperial capital and home of high culture was that now and again life would be disrupted in the most violent manner. The second half of the 1150s had seen Taira battle Minamoto in the city's streets. Three centuries later, for ten years between 1467 and 1477, devastation on a much larger scale came to Kyoto. The Ashikaga *bakufu* used warrior-constables to manage the countryside, much as had the Kamakura *bakufu* before it. Over time, however, these warrior-constables developed their allotted provinces into personal fiefdoms, keeping much of their tax income and building up loyal followings via lord-and-vassal relationships. New regional families emerged, grew in power and became used to squabbling over the shogunal succession – not unlike the courtier families of old vying for influence over the imperial line.

One such dispute in the 1460s saw the Hosokawa and Yamana families go to war, drawing in a great many other families and laying waste, in the process, to large swathes of Kyoto. Much of the fighting was conducted hand-to-hand, through the city's streets and houses. Many of Kyoto's residents fled, and when a bout of fighting ended, their damaged homes fell prey to looters and arsonists. Of the thousands of homes to disappear from Kyoto in the course of what became known as the Ōnin War (1467–77), one was the shogunal palace in the city's Muromachi district. It was a fitting reflection of just how far the shogun's authority had declined.

Worse was to come. At war's end, control over the shogunate fell largely to the Hosokawa family. But it was not the precious prize that it might once have been. Too much power had passed, by now, to provincial warlords. Some of them were former warrior-constables who had taken their provinces for themselves, but many were fresh claimants who made the most of the Ōnin War to displace the old warrior-constables. Most of these emerging warlords, or *daimyō* ('great name'), found themselves able to ignore any orders coming from the succession of Minamoto puppets that the Hosokawa installed as shogun.

The Ōnin War marked the beginning of the Sengoku or 'Warring States' period in Japan. More than a hundred warlords across the country strove to defend and expand their fiefdoms or 'domains' and to gain new vassals: by fighting, spying, strategising, making fragile alliances and producing codes of conduct for what, to all intents and purposes, were mini-kingdoms. For the next century, Japan had no true political centre. As with the decline of aristocratic power hundreds of years before, the most potent unifying force in the country was its culture, which continued to attract from the samurai class both real connoisseurs and canny social climbers.

One evening in 1560, a young warlord named Oda Nobunaga, from Owari province, performed some steps from the Nō play *Atsumori*, written by Zeami and based on the story from *The Tale of the Heike* about the fateful meeting of the

Minamoto warrior Kumagai no Naozane and his Taira rival. It was by way of preparation for the battle to come: the next morning, Nobunaga mounted a surprise attack on a rival warlord, Imagawa Yoshimoto, and defeated him. He went on to win a series of further victories, allying himself with a warlord named Matsudaira (later 'Tokugawa') Ieyasu along the way and in 1568 found himself at the gates of Kyoto.

Nobunaga dreamed of unifying Japan under his rule, but he did not seek the title of shogun. Instead, he used his power to ensure that the office went to his favoured candidate, Ashikaga Yoshiaki. Nobunaga built him a castle in the Muromachi district, as a means of keeping him both safe and under close surveillance – at least in theory. In fact, Yoshiaki became so upset at his humiliating status as Nobunaga's plaything that in 1572 he sought an alliance with Takeda Shingen, lord of Kai province and an arch-enemy of Nobunaga. Early in 1573, Takeda's forces overwhelmed those of Nobunaga and his ally Tokugawa Ieyasu at the Battle of Mikatagahara. Fortunately for Nobunaga, Takeda – the 'Lion of Kai' – fell fatally ill or injured shortly thereafter and his forces began to return home. Nobunaga spent the months that followed mopping up some of his remaining enemies in central Honshū and bringing the Ashikaga shogunate to a final, ignominious end by forcing Yoshiaki from power and into exile.

In Kyoto, Nobunaga bought himself some goodwill from the imperial court by paying to have palaces and shrines patched up. Many were in a sorry state after long decades of on-and-off warfare and the comparative poverty, by this point, of the imperial family. It was said that when Japan's 103rd emperor, Go-Tsuchimikado, died in 1500, his body lay for six weeks in a room in the imperial palace until enough donations came in to pay for a funeral.

Even with the imperial family largely onside, however, Nobunaga still faced the considerable power of Japan's Buddhist establishment. He had made swift work of the Tendai sect already, sending 30,000 men up Mount Hiei in 1571 to destroy its sprawling temple complex and sub-temples and to murder its monks along with the ordinary men, women and children who called the mountain home. Shinran's True Pure Land sect, by contrast, proved difficult to dislodge. It had grown enormously in numbers and influence, and its patriarch, Kennyo, lived in a heavily fortified complex in Osaka, known as the Ishiyama Hongan-ji. From there, he denounced Nobunaga as an enemy of the Buddhist law, issuing a call to arms that resulted in uprisings across central Honshū.

For all his later reputation as a bloodthirsty warlord, pitiless in the taking even of innocent life, Oda Nobunaga was also a master strategist who understood perhaps better than anyone else how to deploy the forces and technology available to him. By the time of the Sengoku era, the choreographed samurai engagements of old had given way to warfare on a much larger scale, making heavier use than in the past of trained peasants serving as foot-soldiers, or *ashigaru*. Some fought with longbows made from bamboo and rattan. Others wielded pikes, or else carried essential supplies – from food to the conch-shell trumpets and drums used in battle.

The importance of *ashigaru* was heightened by the arrival of firearms in Japan, brought by the earliest known Europeans to set foot in the country: Portuguese traders, the first of whom arrived by mistake in 1543 when stormy weather forced their Chinese vessel on to the shores of the Japanese island of Tanegashima. Within months of the first Portuguese arquebus being brought ashore, modified copies were being made and distributed to warlord armies. They were not especially accurate, but they required far less training to use than a sword or a bow and arrow. Bulletproof armour quickly became a must-have for samurai. The ideal armourer, it was said, was one who would mourn more deeply even than his client's own family should he succumb to a bullet that ought never to have struck flesh. A reliable suit of armour was one that already had a dent in it, either from a gunshot test carried out by its maker or from a bullet fired on the battlefield.

In contrast to the splendid, ornate suits of armour that survive from later eras of peace, designed for gift and display rather than fighting, armour in the Sengoku era was simple, strong and sometimes rather ugly – including parts recycled from battlefield leftovers. The only exceptions might be a colourful horned or feathered helmet and the banner (*sashimono*) affixed to the back of the armour, bearing the emblem (*mon*) of the samurai's lord. *Mon* designs were often based on plants, animals or geometric shapes. The imperial family's *mon* was a chrysanthemum, while that of the Tokugawa family featured three hollyhock leaves inside a circle.

Much of Nobunaga's reputation as a smart and determined strategist rests on the Battle of Nagashino in 1575 and his drawn-out efforts to take the Ishiyama Hongan-ji by force. Nagashino was a castle located in territory belonging to Tokugawa Ieyasu, which in 1575 faced a siege by the forces of Takeda Shingen's son and successor, Katsuyori.

Nobunaga led 30,000 men against Katsuyori, outnumbering his forces by two to one and using – according to an impressive but disputed account of the fighting – a pioneering firearms technique. He set up a stockade and placed 3,000 of his best arquebusiers behind it, dividing them into three rotating ranks so that when Katsuyori's cavalry began their charge they were met with almost constant fire.

Nobunaga followed his victory at Nagashino with an attack on the Ishiyama Hongan-ji. He had his troops destroy crops in the surrounding fields in an effort to starve the enemy into submission. When Kennyo struck a deal with a *daimyō* at the south-western end of Honshū to supply the Hongan-ji by sea, Nobunaga is said to have had seven ships built whose wooden frames were clad with protective metal plates. In this way, he gained command of the sea around the Hongan-ji and was able by 1580 to force Kennyo's surrender.

Unopposed now in central Honshū, Nobunaga had his sights set on south-western Honshū and the islands of Shikoku and Kyūshū. But in a turn of events worthy of its own Nō play, Nobunaga was betrayed by one of his generals, Akechi Mitsuhide. At dawn on 21 June 1582, Nobunaga and his men found themselves surrounded in the Honnō-ji temple in Kyoto, where they were staying for the night. Nobunaga kept fighting as his men fell around him and the temple began to burn. At last, injured, he retired to a back room and performed *seppuku*, cutting open his belly to free his spirit.

Akechi Mitsuhide's victory over his former lord was short-lived. Within a fortnight of Oda Nobunaga's death, another of his generals, Toyotomi Hideyoshi, had hunted Akechi down and claimed the mantle of Nobunaga's successor. It was a remarkable moment for a man who had started out as a lowly peasant soldier, carrying Nobunaga's sandals and putting up with being called Saru ('Monkey'). This rapid rise perhaps contributed to Hideyoshi's extraordinary ambition. He dreamed of one day conquering Korea, China and even far-away India, even sending bold and threatening letters to the Spanish in Manila. Indeed, whereas Nobunaga had been on generally friendly terms with Portuguese traders and Jesuit missionaries in Japan, Hideyoshi quickly began to regard them with suspicion.

Europe's role in Japanese affairs had its origins in the rise of the Portuguese and Spanish maritime empires, beginning in the late 1400s. The Treaty of Tordesillas (1494) had drawn an imaginary line down the Atlantic, roughly halfway between the Cape Verde Islands off the West African coast and the lands reached by Christopher Columbus in the course of his famous voyages. The Spanish were granted everything to the west of that line and the Portuguese everything to the east, allowing their merchant ships to explore trading possibilities in East Africa, India, Malacca and, by the late 1550s, Macau in southern China.

The accidental arrival of the Portuguese on the island of Tanegashima in 1543 opened the way for what became a very lucrative trade running between China and Japan. The two countries had been trading on and off for centuries, but the Portuguese had the good fortune to arrive at a point where trade had all but ceased because of the chaos of the Sengoku era and problems with piracy. They were delighted to find that raw Chinese silk would fetch up to ten times its purchase price in Japan, alongside demand in China for Japanese exports including silver. They even found a market in Japan for European or *nanban* attire – the word meant 'southern barbarians' and was applied to the Portuguese because they reached Japan from a southerly direction.

Much of the Portuguese trade ran between southern China and ports in Kyūshū, where it proved attractive to local *daimyō* in search of new sources of tax income. Jesuit missionaries, led initially by Francis Xavier in 1549, made the most of the situation, suggesting to these *daimyō* that if they allowed missions to operate in their domains then missionaries might be able to persuade their merchant compatriots to choose their ports for the China–Japan trade. Some combination of financial incentives and the attractiveness of the missionaries' religious message – after several false starts caused by cultural and linguistic misunderstandings – led to several *daimyō* and their vassals becoming Christians.

This state of affairs seems not to have troubled Oda Nobunaga. It was taking place in a part of Japan that was not yet under his control, and when it came to religious enemies the Buddhists of Mount Hiei and the Ishiyama Hongan-ji represented a far more pressing threat. Hideyoshi, on the other hand, was appalled to learn in 1586, when he arrived in Kyūshū to bring the powerful Shimazu clan to heel, that the entire coastal town of Nagasaki lay in Jesuit hands, having been gifted to them by the local *daimyō*.

Facing a massive army of some 200,000 men, the Shimazu capitulated in 1587. Hideyoshi proceeded to take Nagasaki back from the Jesuits, giving them twenty days to leave Japan and take their 'pernicious' doctrine of Christianity with them. He eventually changed his mind, regarding the Portuguese ships that traded between China and Japan – and also across to India and Europe – as too important to risk disrupting. Besides, Hideyoshi was known to be a fan of *nanban* fashion, which included capes, trousers and hats, alongside crosses and rosaries worn about the body. The Jesuits had, however, been put on notice, along with their convert congregations.

Given though Hideyoshi was to self-aggrandisement, from having himself pictured as a Chinese emperor in a screen painting to arranging for Nō plays to be written about his achievements (and then starring in them), he was also both serious and practical in planning for the reunification of Japan. His last remaining enemies by 1590 were the Hōjō family, who decided to make their stand against Hideyoshi by calling all their allies to come to defend Odawara Castle in the Kantō region of eastern Honshū. Hideyoshi did not so much lay siege to the castle as invite his armies to temporarily relocate to the surrounding area. There they enjoyed music and sumo wrestling, spent time with their wives, tended little vegetable gardens, took part in tea ceremonies and generally had a fine old time within sight of the slowly starving inhabitants of the castle. Hideyoshi also took the opportunity to invite the *daimyō* of northern Japan down to Odawara to pledge their allegiance, meaning that when in August 1590 the Hōjō finally surrendered, Hideyoshi controlled the whole country: Honshū, Shikoku and Kyūshū. Only much later would the large island of Ezo (now Hokkaidō) to the north of Honshū come to be considered part of Japan.

Hideyoshi now proceeded to shuffle fiefdoms around, in

order to reward, punish and keep in check potential rivals. He instituted what was effectively a hostage system, whereby family members of *daimyō* were required to stay at his residence in Momoyama, near Kyoto. And he initiated a 'sword hunt', confiscating weapons held by the peasantry so that tilling the land might once again become their only concern in life. Peasants were forbidden, under new regulations, not just from taking up arms but from making career changes of any kind. Only samurai might now wear swords, and they were required to live in the castle towns that were rapidly becoming the centre of economic life in each domain. Land surveys were carried out to determine a basis for tax, and measures were standardised across Japan.

In a great age of castle-building, Hideyoshi was responsible for the creation of three: Osaka Castle was built on the site where the Ishiyama Hongan-ji had once stood; Jurakutei was erected in Kyoto, on the site of the first imperial palace; and Fushimi was constructed just south-east of Kyoto in 1593–4. Intended as a modest retirement villa for Hideyoshi, this last grew into an impressive castle on which a quarter of a million men were said to have worked and whose *donjon*, or keep, stood on enormous stone foundations and rose five storeys high – each featuring curved wooden eaves topped by tiles. Within Fushimi's walls, space was made for a mini 'Mountain Village' consisting of gardens, fruit trees, a stream for boating, two tea-houses, moon-viewing platforms and a number of Nō stages. Castle interiors were no less splendid. Their walls were often decorated with gold and silver leaf, along with screens painted by masters of the legendary Kanō school.

Where Oda Nobunaga's triumphs a few years earlier had been ruined by treason, Hideyoshi's were eaten away at by his own vanity and worsening paranoia: He launched two disastrous invasions of Korea in 1592 and 1597, causing enormous loss of life and lasting bitterness towards Japan; He had twenty-six Christians crucified in 1597 because he had come to believe that missionaries were preparing the ground for a Spanish invasion of Japan; and he took to killing or forcing suicide upon anyone who challenged him or came bearing bad news. At least one messenger was sawn in half.

Prominent among the casualties of Hideyoshi's late career were his own nephew Hidetsugu and the tea-master Sen no Rikyū. Having given the tea ceremony in Japan its classic form, Rikyū had become tea-master first to Oda Nobunaga and then subsequently to Hideyoshi. He appears to have served Hideyoshi as a political advisor of sorts, too, taking part in peace negotiations with important families like the Shimazu. For reasons that no one fully understands, Rikyū fell from favour with Hideyoshi and in 1591 was ordered to take his own life. This the ageing tea-master did after serving tea to some friends one final time, while 3,000 soldiers surrounded his tea-house. Even this was not enough for Hideyoshi, who had a statue of Rikyū taken from its home in a Zen temple and publicly crucified.

By the middle of 1598, it was clear that Hideyoshi was dying. Sacred *kagura* dances were offered for his health, sponsored by the imperial court. Prayers were said in temples and shrines across Kyoto. The man himself, meanwhile, appeared to be preparing for the end. He sent parting gifts to the emperor and ordered important *daimyō* to attend him and swear their allegiance to his infant son, Hideyori. Soon after, Hideyoshi died, leaving behind a final poem:

> My life
> Came like dew
> Disappears like dew.
> All of Naniwa
> Is dream after dream.

Power in Japan, until Toyotomi Hideyori came of age, lay in the hands of a Council of Five Elders. Among them was Tokugawa Ieyasu, who had acquiesced to Hideyoshi's seizure of power after the death of Oda Nobunaga rather than embracing it with much enthusiasm. Hideyoshi had been well aware of Ieyasu's feelings, and as part of his reshuffling of fiefdoms had sought to move the Tokugawa family safely away from Kyoto, sending them east. The strategy proved not entirely successful. At 2.5 million *koku* – *koku* being an expression of a domain's wealth in terms of rice production – the new Tokugawa lands were the largest of any *daimyō*, larger even than Hideyoshi's own. The Tokugawa castle town of Edo began to develop rapidly, reflecting Ieyasu's fortunes, administrative skills and rising ambitions.

Those ambitions were kept in check for no more than a few months after Hideyoshi's death, at which point tensions within the council became clear. Out in the country, *daimyō* began to gather around either Tokugawa Ieyasu or the interests of Toyotomi Hideyori. The two sides clashed at the Battle of Sekigahara in October 1600: an eastern coalition fighting for Ieyasu and a western one for Hideyori. It was the largest battle ever fought between two groups of samurai, with per-haps 100,000 men on each side – albeit amid fog, mud and a certain amount of artful waiting and watching by generals keen to see which way the battle might go, it is possible that only a fraction of that number actually entered the fray.

Ieyasu triumphed at Sekigahara and had himself appoint-ed shogun in 1603, passing power to his son Hidetada two years later. From behind the scenes, Ieyasu continued the work of building his new regime. He initiated the largest redistribution of land in Japanese history, rewarding loyal allies (*fudai daimyō*, or 'inner lords') while cutting those who had opposed him at Sekigahara down to size: confiscating land and completely dissolving nearly ninety warrior houses. Formerly hostile lords who survived this purge came to be known as *tozama daimyō* ('outer lords') and were treated with caution over the decades that followed.

Ieyasu's greatest remaining problem was Osaka Castle, where Hideyori and his mother were surrounded by sam-urai who were either personally loyal to them or deeply op-posed to the Tokugawa family – around 90,000 men in total. Ieyasu took his time. He first ensured that the imperial court in Kyoto would not involve itself in warrior affairs any longer. The danger was that Hideyori be granted some imperial title, such as regent, which would strengthen his claim against Ieyasu. Rather than playing politics, court nobles were urged to be 'diligent in their studies', while the emperor's role in the nation's affairs was confined to ritual and the arts. At last, in 1614, Ieyasu considered the time right to launch an assault on Osaka Castle. This he did, but it was testament to the castle's design that 90,000 people inside were able to hold off a force double that size. It took until the summer of the next year for the castle to fall, at which point Hideyori and his mother took their own lives.

Tokugawa Ieyasu's plan for a unified Japan revolved around a *bakuhan* system: a blend of the old *bakufu* (warrior 'tent government') system with the more recent *han*, or domain system. In practice, this meant that regional *daimyō* enjoyed all but unfettered power within their own domains, provided that they abided by a 'Code for the Military Houses' issued by the new Tokugawa shogunate in 1615 and regularly updated. This included a ban on harbouring enemies of the shogunate, a ban on building new castles, an insistence that intended repairs to existing castles be notified to the shogunate, a requirement to inform the shogunate of plots or factions in neighbouring domains, the seeking of permission before marriages involving *daimyō* were contracted and the living of a frugal and studious life, to include practice of the martial arts. Hideyoshi's hostage system was formalised and somewhat sanitised as *sankin-kōtai*, or 'alternate attendance': *daimyō* lived in Edo every other year and left their families behind when they moved back to their domains.

Ieyasu personally understood hostage systems all too well, having lived as a hostage for much of his childhood. Its security and surveillance advantages were obvious, but it had other bonuses besides. Maintaining two homes – one in Edo, and one back in one's own domain – and then paying for regular travel in full retinue, was very expensive. The shogunate also required feudal lords to chip in for repairs to temples, roads and other elements of Japan's ravaged infrastructure, meaning that potential rivals were effectively prevented from building up too much wealth and power. They were free, of course, to tax their own people more severely. But that would risk anger and instability, weakening their position still further.

The distinction between samurai and commoners, established by Hideyoshi, was now maintained and elaborated through a four-tier class system. At the top were the samurai, making up around 8 per cent of the population. Next came farmers, artisans and finally merchants – lowliest of all on the basis that they dealt in the produce of others rather than producing anything themselves. This rather moralistic approach to running Japanese society was a major feature of the Tokugawa settlement. Under the influence of Neo-Confucian thought, emphasis was placed on order, on each person knowing their place – extending to rules on what peasants were permitted to wear, and how they might spend their free time – and on the right and duty of rulers to engage in the moral education and betterment of the masses. Family, frugality and obedience were all highly prized, and featured heavily in the rhetoric used in Tokugawa edicts.

All of this only worked, of course, if a basic unity, once achieved, could be maintained. Having emerged victorious at Sekigahara, forced the imperial court into submission, shuffled warlords around and then dispensed with Hideyoshi's would-be successor, the House of Tokugawa might have regarded itself as reasonably safe. Abroad, Ieyasu looked forward to developing trading relationships with the Spanish in Manila and the Americas, alongside the English and Dutch East India Companies. He even appeared well-disposed towards Japanese Christians, whose numbers by 1606 may have been as high as 300,000 out of a population of 15 or 18 million people. Over the 1610s and 1620s, however, Ieyasu's successors came to see Christianity increasingly as Hideyoshi had: as an alien and unwelcome force in Japanese life, and potentially a political threat, too – a view encouraged by English and Dutch claims that Portugal and Spain were plotting an invasion of Japan. The final straw came in 1637 when an otherwise secure shogunate found itself facing a threat from a most unexpected quarter.

The rugged, pine-hill countryside of Shimabara domain, around 25 miles east of Nagasaki, was under the control of a *daimyō* called Matsukura Katsuie. He and his father had become infamous of late for squeezing high taxes out of local farmers and visiting particularly nasty punishments on those who couldn't or wouldn't pay. One was known as the 'Mino dance': a farmer would be dressed in his winter straw coat, have his hands tied behind his back and then the coat would be set on fire. Others were thrown into snake pits, sliced with bamboo saws or boiled in sulphurous hot springs. Things were made worse by a series of poor harvests between 1634 and 1637, to which the usual response from a domain lord would be a reduction in the tax requirement for that year. That wasn't the way that the Matsukura family did things: leaving some in their domain reduced to eating mud and straw.

To this dry tinder in Shimabara was added a spark in December 1637. Some accounts suggest that a farmer in Arima village was forced to watch while his daughter was tortured by some of Matsukura's men. Either this poor farmer, or others in the village, ended up killing her torturers, starting a rebellion that spread to other villages nearby. Within a few weeks, as many as 23,000 people out of a population of 45,000 in Shimabara domain joined the rebellion. A similar uprising began out in the nearby Amakusa islands.

Many of those involved in what became known as the Shimabara Rebellion were Christian, and at some point a devout and charismatic young man known as Amakusa Shirō became a figurehead for them. It was said that he could call down birds from the sky to sit on his hand (recalling Francis of Assisi) and that he had been seen walking on the water just off the Shimabara peninsula. Religion, hunger, deep grievance and a number of disgruntled *rōnin* – masterless samurai – came together to create a very serious problem for Shimabara's leaders, as somewhere between 20,000 and 60,000 rebels took over and fortified the abandoned remains of Hara Castle, above which a Christian flag was flown bearing the words 'Praise Be the Most Holy Sacrament' in Portuguese. On three sides of the castle, cliffs dropped down into the Pacific Ocean, while on the approachable side the outer wall stood some thirty metres high and had in front of it a large area of difficult, marshy ground.

The rebels were untrained, and though some had firearms and swords most were equipped only with sickles, scythes and home-made spears. They ought to have been no match for samurai drawn from several nearby domains and led by a general named Itakura Shigemasa, dispatched from Edo to bring the incident swiftly to an end. But three successive attacks failed, as did Itakura's other measures. He sent ninjas into Hara Castle as spies, but at least one of them was caught because he didn't understand the local dialect or some of the

Portuguese Christian words being used. He got labourers to build towers with artillery emplacements to help his forces get closer to the castle. That didn't work either: some of the rebels started stoning the labourers, who complained rather indignantly to the rebels that they were just doing their jobs. Itakura's forces even tried digging under the castle, only for the rebels to fill the tunnels with smoke, faeces and urine. Then, in mid-February, Itakura himself was shot in the head and killed.

All this was highly embarrassing for the shogunate. How could a peasant rabble be holding off a samurai army? In the second half of February, Itakura's replacement, Matsudaira Nobutsuna, launched a siege of the castle, backed by an expanded Tokugawa force of between 100,000 and 150,000 men. Word was sent to a Dutch merchant vessel, the *De Ryp*, based at the port of Hirado, to come and bombard Hara Castle with more modern ordnance than the Tokugawa forces possessed. Yet again, things did not go to plan. Around 400 cannonballs were fired across a period of two weeks, but many sailed over the castle and landed amid the Tokugawa forces. Some of the rebels then fired arrows carrying paper messages at the Tokugawa army, taunting them for requiring the help of foreigners to fight their battles. The Dutch were quietly asked to leave, and the siege went on.

In the end, hunger took its toll. By April, supplies of food and ammunition were so low in the castle that a group led by Amakusa Shirō left under cover of darkness to see what they could steal from the Tokugawa encampment. They were spotted – the burning wicks of their matchlocks gave them away – and hundreds were killed. It was clear from the look of their corpses when day broke that malnutrition was setting in at Hara Castle. One source suggests that their stomachs were cut open to get a look at their most recent meal. It was just seaweed, barley and leaves. Not a single stomach had rice in it. This was the cue for an all-out attack on the castle, during which samurai scaled the castle walls in full armour – according, in any case, to screen paintings of the siege. The battle lasted two or three days, as half-starved rebels tried to fight off their attackers using cooking pots and cauldrons. In the end, everyone in the castle was put to death – women and children included – bar just a few people who somehow managed to escape.

The Shimabara Rebellion was a shock for the shogunate: a reminder of how grievances could combine to bring disparate groups of people together and threaten the legitimacy of the new regime. Official accounts of the rebellion claimed that Christianity, *rōnin* and foreign interference were primarily to blame: an attempt to pass Shimabara off as an aberration – a legacy of Portuguese and Spanish meddling in Kyūshū and very much the kind of thing that *daimyō* elsewhere, who might be inclined to rebel, should *not* expect to be possible in their own domains.

This version of events sat well alongside genuine worries about the threat posed by Christianity and the Iberian powers to Japan's still-fragile unity. Those fears resulted in a series of *sakoku* ('closed country') edicts being issued between 1633 and 1639. Japanese were forbidden to leave the country without permission, on pain of death if and when they returned. A ban was placed on the import of European and especially Christian books. The clampdown on Christianity was tightened, with rewards offered for tip-offs about 'hidden Christians'. Foreign trade was confined to Nagasaki, where it could be controlled by the shogunate. Portuguese and Spanish missionaries and traders were to have no further role in Japan's affairs. Instead, the Dutch became the sole European power permitted to trade with Japan, operating from 1641 from a small man-made island called Dejima, connected to the Nagasaki coast by a small stone bridge that was guarded at all times.

Future generations of Japanese would wonder about the wisdom of cutting themselves off from so much of the world in this way, even if links were maintained with China, Korea and parts of South-East Asia. At the time, however, the logic was clear. The process of unifying Japan had been made more difficult and bloody than it needed to be by foreigners playing politics and by the outsized influence of religious interests, Buddhist and Christian. A period of stability was called for, and for a couple of centuries the Tokugawa shogunate largely provided it. Nor did stability necessarily entail boredom. If one had a little time and money to spare, Japan during its period of early modern peace could be a very entertaining place indeed.

# CHAPTER 6

# The Life of the City

Anyone who doubted the power of the new Tokugawa regime in the early 1600s needed only to look on as vast quantities of stone and timber, alongside valuable metals like gold, silver, copper and iron were shipped into the shogunal capital of Edo at the expense of newly quiescent *daimyō* around the country. A building boom was underway, on such a scale that early modern environmentalists began to fear for the future of Japan's forests. An ambitious network of new urban waterways was meanwhile being dug; once complete, these waterways, lined with thriving shops and restaurants, would transport goods around the growing city. Of the various new bridges built over Edo's rivers and canals, the grandest was Nihonbashi, the 'Japan Bridge', completed in 1604 and soon playing host to a famous fish market. The endpoint of these waterways was Edo Bay, from where a network of shipping routes connected rapidly developing ports around the coasts of Honshū, Kyūshū and Shikoku.

Looking back at Edo from the bay, the city's skyline was dominated by Edo Castle. Here, too, Japan's *daimyō* contributed materials and manpower. Some 300,000 men laboured on the castle at any given time, digging moats and building the keep, main court and ramparts – much of it from huge pieces of stone brought in on boats. Tokugawa Ieyasu's son Hidetada was shogun during the main phase of the building work (1605–14) and is said to have made daily progress inspections. Such was the sheer scale of the project, featuring several moated castle areas within the larger castle complex – intended as separate accommodation for a retired shogun, a serving shogun and a successor – that even the task of keeping an eye on things was rather taxing. Tea-rooms had to be established at various points around the site, whose perimeter may have been up to ten miles in length, so that Hidetada might refresh himself.

Some *daimyō* maintained homes within the castle walls. Others lived atop the seven hills that stood to the north and west of the castle, vying with one another to build impressive residences worthy of their status. That status was measured in terms of the productivity of their lands. One *koku* of rice was notionally enough to feed an adult male for a year, and the minimum qualification for a *daimyō* was to have 10,000 *koku* to his name. Mōri domain in south-western Honshū was valued at 369,000 *koku*. Tokugawa lands were now valued at in excess of 3 million *koku*. A samurai's annual stipend would likewise be paid in *koku*, depending on his rank.

The buildings and immaculately landscaped gardens of the 'high city' estates, the most lavishly appointed of which marked a return to the heyday of Heian courtier homes, were protected from prying eyes and would-be attackers or thieves by substantial walls. Into these were set gates whose dimensions were laid out in law according to each *daimyō*'s status. Add to these estates the land required for the homes of Tokugawa retainers, and around 70 per cent of Edo was claimed by samurai of one kind or another. Shrines and temples took up a further 15 per cent of the city's real estate, most notably three large temple complexes at Ueno, Shiba and Asakusa. Their primary purpose was to protect the city according to the same Chinese geomantic ideas that had been used in the planning of Kyoto many centuries before.

That left only 15 per cent for the dwellings and businesses of Edo's townspeople, some in the valleys that separated the hills of the high city but most in the 'low city' to the south and east of the castle and bordering Edo Bay. A great deal had to be done with this space, such was the demand for traders, artisans and craftspeople of all kinds, from tailors to tatami-mat makers. Dwellings in these parts of the city were comparatively modest, but they benefited from the construction boom going on elsewhere in Edo and around the country. The late 1500s and early 1600s witnessed the founding or expansion of castle towns around Japan, including Osaka, Okayama, Tokushima, Kōchi, Fukuoka and Kumamoto. Their importance grew after 1600 as samurai withdrew from the countryside and took up residence in the castle towns of their lords, serving them now more as bureaucrats than spillers of blood. All this building work yielded improved techniques, which made their way down the social scale to the homes of humble townspeople. They might have been small, but increasingly they would have strong stone foundations alongside higher-quality and more precisely measured components of wood and bamboo.

These commoner homes tended to be long and narrow, since space fronting on to the street was at a premium. Inside, one found the essentials of life: a hearth, food, cooking utensils and drinking water brought into the city via a vast network of aqueducts and wooden pipes, regularly upgraded during the seventeenth century as the city's population grew. In lieu of a sewage system, human waste was collected and sold as fertilizer. Waste from samurai households was the most valuable, since it was assumed that their better diets would yield a nutrient-rich end product. The trade was so valuable that in Osaka fights had been known to break out among farmers over collection rights and prices. In Edo, the entrepreneurial spirit stretched even to the idea of placing receptacles in the street so that the urine of passers-by might be collected and then sold on. The authorities denied the request.

Frustration at the authorities was a prominent theme in Edo life. A combination of pragmatism during the shogunate's precarious early decades and Neo-Confucian ideals about rulers making benevolent interventions in people's lives led Japan's leaders to seek to manage everyday affairs to an extent rarely if ever before attempted. Much revolved around the strict social hierarchy that had its roots in Hideyoshi's disarming of the peasantry and which had since been articulated and enforced by the Tokugawa shoguns. Amid the bustle of any Edo street, society's samurai elite would stand out thanks to their swords, silk clothing – colour and quality determined by the individual's status – and their top-knot hairstyles, featuring a shaved pate. In addition to the casual surveillance mounted by samurai out shopping or going for a stroll, one found the early modern equivalent of police boxes dotted around the city: there to keep an eye out for petty crime or the fights that occasionally broke out between gangsters or samurai from feuding families.

The regulations against which a person's behaviour might be judged meanwhile multiplied, from frequently restated bans on dumping rubbish in rivers or canals to strict controls on travel. The alternate attendance system did much to develop Japan's road networks, as *daimyō* and their families journeyed to and from Edo in vast retinues. The busiest route was the 350-mile-long Tōkaidō (Eastern Sea Route), connecting Kyoto with Edo and lined at points along the way with shops, inns and restaurants. Bends were built into these roads so that they could not easily be used by armies in the event of an uprising against the Tokugawa. Ordinary Japanese, however, had to have a very good reason to leave their village or town. Official travel documents needed to be obtained and shown at various stages of any journey, leading to a boom in religious pilgrimage as one of relatively few purposes for which travel was considered acceptable. It was a testament to their seriousness on this point that the shogunate went as far as destroying bridges to help funnel travellers through properly policed road networks.

Being discovered outside your village or neighbourhood without good reason was just one among a number of crimes for which the punishment could be severe. Others included allowing your house to catch fire – a particular threat in densely packed cities like Edo, where a devastating fire in 1657 killed a fifth of the population, did terrible damage to Edo Castle and destroyed many hundreds of homes.

To go by the era's edicts alone, farmers lived a comparatively mundane existence. They dressed in clothes of hemp or cotton, ate wheat, Deccan grass and potatoes rather than rice or noodles and were forbidden from drinking tea or *sake* on the grounds that these things were inappropriate to their lowly station. They tilled the land by day and even had their free time in the evenings planned for them by the shogunate: making rope and sacks. The best way to control the peasantry, it was thought, was to allow them enough food to keep them active in the fields and prevent them absconding to a neighbouring domain but not *so* much that they risked becoming lazy. In practice, this could mean 50 per cent or more of a person's agricultural yield being taken in tax. When times were hard, wives or daughters might be sold off, or else entire families would find themselves tipped into vagrancy.

In practice, wealthier farmers enjoyed a modest amount of freedom. Japan's 63,000 villages were largely self-governing, and provided that the required amount of tax in rice was produced then a village might be spared too many unpleasant visits by the samurai tasked with its oversight. If they owned their land, farmers stood to benefit from rising agricultural yields. They might also be involved in the production, on the side, of goods like silk, paper, lacquer, cotton, rapeseed, indigo and tea. As Japan became more connected, particular foods and products emerged as well-known regional specialities, and were in demand around the country. They could be bartered or exchanged for regional currencies issued in paper, or Japan's new national currency, issued in gold, silver and later copper.

The great hub for the exchange of goods and currencies was Osaka, with its enormous port whose intricate waterways were lined with warehouses. Alongside Edo, Kyoto and Nagasaki, Osaka was considered important enough for the shogunate to retain direct control, as it did over the country's largest precious-metals mines. All three cities reached a considerable size by 1700. Osaka was home to around 400,000 people and Kyoto to half a million. Edo meanwhile grew to become at that time perhaps the largest city on Earth, home to around a million people.

Even in a time of peace, one of the foremost responsibilities of the samurai was to study the making of war. Far more was done during the Edo period than in the preceding Warring States era to develop and codify various martial techniques, from horsemanship and swordsmanship to the arts of stealth, judo and even swimming. The very concept of 'martial arts' in Japan dates not from times of war but from the first century of peace after 1600.

Samurai in a city like Edo might also study other sorts of arts besides, including music. Centuries-old court music known as *gagaku* was revived and codified in this era, and warriors learned to play its primary instruments: lute (*biwa*), mouth organ (*shō*), flute (*fue*) and a double-reeded wind instrument called *hichiriki*. Other approved pastimes for warriors, similarly rooted in Japan's aristocratic past, included flower-arranging, calligraphy, painting and the tea ceremony. There were also the joys of shopping, as Edo grew into a giant emporium for goods coming in from all over Japan and even further afield. Bookshops were an important part of this picture, offering works encompassing cookery, medicine, poetry, drama and satirical fiction. Guidebooks were popular, too: bluffer's guides to the high arts, for townsmen on the up, or travel books for people who had their documentation in order and were about to make a much-anticipated trip to a famous city, temple or shrine.

Edo's restaurants, proliferating from the mid-1600s, must now and again have been a challenge for samurai morals. When it came to food, Tokugawa Ieyasu had been notably abstemious, preferring simple barley and rice as his staple and recommending the same to his men. But Edo was soon home to culinary innovations from across Japan and beyond. One could try red and white fishcake, soup flavoured with chrysanthemum, carp and sea bass prepared according to secret recipes, various kinds of sushi and soba and a delicious-sounding Dutch dish made from minced beef and cabbage, mixed with egg and wine and fried in breadcrumbs.

All these enjoyments were as nothing compared with the beating heart of Edo's social life: the Yoshiwara district, relocated to the outskirts of the city after the great fire of 1657 and packed with tea-houses, bath-houses and theatres. Each of Japan's major cities had its own pleasure quarters, where samurai and wealthy townsmen could exchange the rule-bound drudgery of everyday life for a world of drama and fantasy. People called it the 'floating world', or *ukiyo*: a Buddhist term for the melancholy reality of impermanence, repurposed now to capture the ephemeral, dreamlike quality of the thrills available in a place like Yoshiwara.

Entering Yoshiwara, one didn't so much leave rules and hierarchy behind as exchange an old set for a new one. Money rather than social status was what counted, particularly when it came to arranging entertainment from one of the district's thousands of courtesans. At the lower end of the scale were country girls forced by circumstances to sell sex. At the upper end, a courtesan might be the daughter of a samurai, lavishly accoutred and able to sing, dance, play a musical instrument, tell stories and engage in some suitably restrained repartee with her clients. Out of the latter tradition, geisha emerged in the second half of the 1700s. The word meant 'person of accomplishment', and the first generation were men. Women later took over the role, and an imperfectly observed distinction took hold whereby the highest tier of courtesans might offer sexual services while geisha would not.

Should a man find himself in the rarefied company of either a high-class courtesan or a geisha, merely being rich would not be enough. He had to know how to behave. He required a little preparation to appreciate the musical entertainment on offer and to understand the references on which a geisha's conversation might turn. For the uninitiated, a friend in the know could be very valuable. Failing that, one could buy a book on how to survive and thrive in a pleasure district.

One of the great attractions of these pleasure districts was a form of theatre that emerged right at the beginning of the Tokugawa era. It was said to have its origins in a female dance troupe led by a woman named Okuni, which gained notoriety in the early 1600s for performing eccentric dances alongside comedy sketches poking fun at men visiting brothels. Similar troupes started to appear, many of them put together by brothel-keepers hoping to use the performances to drum up a little business.

The art form came to be called *kabuki*, based on the word *katamuki*, meaning slanted or weird. From very early on, *kabuki* had the potential to inflame people's passions, forcing the shogunate to ban women, and later young men, too, from taking part in the performances. Instead, it was as the preserve of adult males that *kabuki* developed into fully fledged theatre, with stages, curtains, scenery, props and basic story-lines that actors would take as a basis for improvisation. The actor Ichikawa Danjūrō (1660–1704), known for his *aragoto*, or 'rough', acting style, became one of Japan's first bona fide celebrities.

A more scripted type of drama was available in the form of *bunraku*, or puppet theatre. Here, the story was chanted to *shamisen* accompaniment, while puppets of up to two-thirds of life-size acted out the scenes. For all the cleverness of the puppets as their technology advanced, including changeable facial expressions and extraordinary acrobatic feats, a *bunraku* play would stand or fall on its script. The best-loved playwright of the age was Chikamatsu Monzaemon (1653–1724), known both for dramatisations of historical events and for commentaries on contemporary Japanese life. His works are still performed to this day.

The latter sort of play only worked if one was quick to react to the news. Chikamatsu managed it with a play called *The Love Suicides at Sonezaki*, which was first performed on 20 June 1703, less than a month after the double suicide that inspired it. The story tells of a young soy sauce seller called Tokubei and a nineteen-year-old courtesan named Ohatsu, living in Osaka's pleasure district. Tokubei is in trouble. His employer wants him to marry a relative of his, but Tokubei has refused and must now return the money he received for the girl's dowry. Unfortunately, he has lent the money to an acquaintance of his, who denies all knowledge of having received it.

As Tokubei pours out his troubles, Ohatsu responds: 'Did our promises of love hold only for this world? Others before us have chosen reunion through death.' In hopes of being reborn together in the next life, the narrator tells us, they proceed to the Sonezaki shrine and end their lives:

> No one is there to tell the tale, but the wind that blows through Sonezaki Wood transmits it, and high and low alike gather to pray for these lovers who beyond a doubt will in the future attain Buddhahood. They have become models of true love.

Here, as elsewhere in his plays, Chikamatsu manages to capture the conflicts between duty (*giri*) and human feeling (*ninjō*) that were such a feature of life in the Tokugawa period. So concerned were the authorities with the impact of plays like this that suicide was banned in real life and banished from the stage.

Many of the arts of this era were set up not simply for quiet, passive enjoyment but for active participation of various kinds. *Kabuki* could be a raucous, all-day affair. Books of *bunraku* chants allowed people to try out lines for themselves at home or in company, while cheap woodblock printing made it possible to own an image of your favourite courtesan or *kabuki* actor for little more than the price of a snack. Anyone keen to test their wits could try *haikai*: a form of poetry composition that grew out of an older *renga* ('linked verse') tradition, and which involved a group of people improvising lines in turn.

It was very much in keeping with the spirit of the age that an art like poetry, once associated with Japan's imperial court, should now have fresh life breathed into it by an up-and-coming urban bourgeoisie. One of *haikai*'s greatest names was Ihara Saikaku, who once composed no fewer than 1,000 verses in just twelve hours. Saikaku became known, too, as a pioneering writer of fiction that took the bawdy exploits of townsmen as its inspiration. *The Life of an Amorous Man* (1682), which followed the mixed fortunes of a merchant's son named Yonosuke (literally 'man of the world'), became the first in a genre known as *ukiyo-zōshi*: 'books of the floating world'.

Poetry also helped to fill the gap left by the relative decline of Buddhism in this era. Where life in Japan had once been shaped by large sects like Tendai and Shingon and by potent images of salvation at the hands of Amida Buddha, the Tokugawa shogunate drew intellectual inspiration primarily from Neo-Confucianism, with its emphasis on hierarchy, duty and this-worldly values like diligence, restraint and frugality. Buddhism remained a force in national life, closely watched by a dedicated office of the shogunate. But something of a spiritual void seems to have opened up, which beloved poets like Matsuo Bashō (1644–94) managed to fill.

Born into a lower-ranking warrior family, Bashō chose to devote himself to poetry after his lord died, and he became a *rōnin* while still a young man. Where other poets found subject matter aplenty in Japan's great towns and cities, Bashō preferred to travel. He had a keen sense, no doubt shaped by Buddhism, of the value of wandering free from domestic attachments and of the physical and mental discipline that it took to make long journeys away from popular routes like the Tōkaidō. To live in this way, thought Bashō, is truer to the basic nature of human existence. As he put it in *The Narrow Road to the Deep North* (*Oku no Hosomichi*): 'the journey itself is home'.

*The Narrow Road* was Bashō's memoir of a journey undertaken in 1689, from Edo north towards the top of Honshū and then back south along Japan's western coast.

Written in *haibun* – prose punctuated by *haiku* – it reveals Bashō's encounter with 'nature' in the broadest sense: not just its varied landscapes of pines, lakes and waterfalls, but people, monuments and stories, too, which he discovers as he goes. Reaching the Koromo River, Bashō recalls the presence here, long ago, of the ancient imperial army and later Minamoto forces during the Gempei War. 'I laid out my bamboo hat,' he writes, 'and wept without sense of time.' Then comes a *haiku*:

Summer grass –
All that remains
Of warriors' dreams.

At other points in his journey, Bashō appears to be on the verge of wishing that he had stayed at home:

Iizuka . . . was a crude, shabby place, with straw mats covering a dirt floor. There wasn't even a lamp, so we bedded down by the light of the sunken fireplace. Night came, thunder rolled, rain poured down. The roof leaked over our heads, and I was harassed by fleas and mosquitoes. My old illness cropped up, too, and I almost fainted.

The next day, Bashō found that his 'spirits would not rise' – and yet:

This was a pilgrimage to far places, a resignation to self-abandonment and impermanence. Death might come by the roadside, but that is heaven's will. With those thoughts my spirits recovered a bit [and] I began to step broadly on my way.

Tokugawa Japan reached its commercial and artistic peak in the late seventeenth and early eighteenth centuries. Time in Japan was measured in eras, which changed when a new emperor ascended the throne or when good or bad fortune visited the land. The Genroku era, between 1688 and 1704, thus became synonymous with the fruits of the peace that Tokugawa Ieyasu had imposed on the country back at the start of the seventeenth century. The mid-eighteenth century brought a loosening of restrictions on foreign books coming into Japan, helping 'Dutch studies' to get going: the study of books on subjects like medicine by intrepid Japanese intellectuals who pored over European languages for hours on end trying to work out what was being said. And yet by the latter part of that century, a number of trends were becoming established, which would in time chip away at Ieyasu's great vision for a unified and stable Japan.

The most obvious of those trends was the rise of a merchant elite wealthy enough to place some of the *daimyō* in the shade. The writer Ihara Saikaku lauded what he saw of the entrepreneurial spirit in Japan's big cities, but he noted that all too often 'only silver can produce more silver': many a merchant family fortune rested on their monopoly of some good or service. It was also increasingly common for merchants to lend money to *daimyō* or samurai facing straitened circumstances. This made it all the more difficult for Japan's ruling class to mount effective opposition when merchants began to flout the rules on how flamboyantly they might dress or how lavishly they might build and furnish their homes.

The favoured means of addressing this problem, for the shogunate and for leading intellectuals like Ogyū Sorai

(1666–1728), was for samurai to rediscover the old ideal of frugality. If they spent less, then merchant profits would fall and the proper hierarchy in society would be restored. Ogyū also suggested that the samurai ought to return to the countryside, rekindling the relationship between peasants and samurai away from the distractions of urban life. The shogunate did not adopt Ogyū's ideas, but reforming shoguns like Tokugawa Yoshimune, who served from 1716 to 1745, did what they could to curb the profits of merchants and moneylenders and remind the population as a whole of the virtues of simple, austere living.

Beyond rhetoric, the shogunate's options were limited. If rice prices were set too low, then farmers and samurai suffered, the latter because the value of their stipends declined. Set rice prices too high, and starvation might result, as it did most tragically in the Tenpō famine of the 1830s. Hundreds of thousands of people died and severe unrest erupted across the country, as it became clear that the social contract, the duty of those higher up the hierarchy to protect and show benevolence towards those lower down, was failing. Tensions were meanwhile becoming obvious within the samurai class. Lower-ranking samurai increasingly found their stipends either reduced because of their lords' financial woes or in any case no longer sufficient to provide a decent living for their families. Samurai took up part-time jobs or sold off armour – even daughters – to merchants who were keen to purchase a little of their country's faded glamour.

By the early nineteenth century, some of these samurai found themselves drawn not to invocations of the early Tokugawa heyday under Ieyasu – a favourite theme of the shogunate – but much further back in time to an age of rule by emperors.

An important influence here was a 'National Learning' (*Kokugaku*) school of thought, associated with intellectuals like Motoori Norinaga (1730–1801). He argued that a dry, moralising and overly rationalistic Chinese culture had come to exert too much influence in Japan. There was a need, he thought, to return to the poetry of the *Kojiki* (*Record of Ancient Matters, c.* 712) and Murasaki Shikibu's *Tale of Genji*. One could discover there, he argued, a 'pure Japanese heart' – *yamato-gokoro* – whose emotions were those of the *kami* themselves.

Hirata Atsutane (1776–1843) developed these *Kokugaku* ideas in more explicitly political and pro-imperial directions. The emperor, he claimed, was a manifest *kami*, whose role in Japanese life ought to be one of political as well as ceremonial leadership. The Confucian scholar Aizawa Seishisai (1782–1863) agreed, arguing in his *New Theses* (*Shinron*, 1825) that only the reunification of religion and government in Japan, through the return of the emperor to power, could safeguard against the encroachment of European Christian culture into his country's affairs.

The *New Theses* read like a call-to-arms for a younger generation of samurai who were fed up with what they saw as the lazy and conservative leadership of the country by shogunate and *daimyō* alike. They were also well aware of the low regard in which commoners increasingly held the samurai. Having done precious little fighting for many years, Japan's warrior class risked being viewed simply as parasites, doing little more than swagger, hector and spend, or else – as a popular phrase of the day had it – 'count the nostril hairs' of their superiors.

Ideas like these, doing the rounds of schools and fencing academies attended by young samurai, needed only some great event, some crystallising moment, for them really to take hold. In July 1853, the United States of America provided that moment, in the form of four black-hulled steamships arriving in Edo Bay. The mission was led by Commodore Matthew C. Perry, who bore a lengthy letter from President Millard Fillmore addressed to the emperor. The president sought 'friendship, commerce, a supply of coal and provisions [for American steamships operating in Japan's vicinity] and protection for our shipwrecked people'. Fillmore added that he was asking on behalf of a country that stretched 'from ocean to ocean', was populous, rich in resources and very much in favour of overhauling 'ancient laws' of the type that he suspected might prevent the emperor acceding to his request.

There was an edge to the president's letter, which Commodore Perry emphasised by the manner of its delivery. He was accompanied, when he landed on Japanese soil, by the burliest soldiers and marines he could find aboard his ships, along with two military bands. And he was unequivocal in threatening violent repercussions if his president's requests were not met. Watching this encounter were samurai who had been rushed to the scene by their commanders and who now stood arrayed along the hilltops surrounding Edo Bay. They could not have known that the firearms they held in their hands would, in the United States, mostly be found in museums or attics, or that floating out at sea was enough firepower to flatten Edo. Some surely must, however, have returned to their homes that day with a sense that life was about to change.

# CHAPTER 7

# The Promise and Menace of the West

Commodore Matthew C. Perry was not the first westerner in this era to arrive in Japan seeking friendship and commerce. The Russians beat him to it, but were turned down. The Dutch tried in vain to upgrade their limited arrangement in Nagasaki. And the French began paying visits to the Ryukyu Islands to the south of Kyūshū. The American challenge became important because of the threats made by Perry, backed by his four heavily armed ships; mountainously large to Japanese eyes and spewing evil-looking black smoke. Perry's timing was significant, too: faith in the shogunate's leadership, in Japan's domestic and foreign affairs alike, was already ebbing away.

As rumours swirled of an imminent invasion – to which some responded by fleeing Edo while others went out to buy swords and armour – the shogunate made itself look weaker than ever by casting around for ideas, asking the *daimyō* for their thoughts on how best to respond to the United States. Most recognised that in the short term Japan had little option but to acquiesce to America's demands. A Treaty of Peace and Amity was duly signed in 1854, leading to the opening up of two ports: Shimoda, at the mouth of Edo Bay, and Hakodate on the northern island of Ezo. This, however, was only the beginning. The Americans wanted a full commercial treaty, and their envoy, Townsend Harris, knew exactly how to get it.

For centuries, China's place in the Japanese imagination had been that of a cultural and political big brother: an enormous, ancient empire whose ideas and values were threaded through Japanese life at every level. Nothing could more clearly have demonstrated the threat posed by aggressive, technologically advanced western powers than the humiliation China had experienced at the hands of the British during the First Opium War. Townsend Harris made the most of these events, and the anxiety they caused in Japan, to persuade the shogunate that friendship with America was the best way of ensuring Japan's security. A Treaty of Amity and Commerce was concluded in 1858, under whose terms six Japanese ports were opened up to trade and strict limits were placed on Japanese import tariffs. Americans were permitted to reside in the treaty ports, safe in the knowledge that any crime they committed would be tried under American rather than Japanese law. Similar agreements were soon made with the Russians, British, French and Dutch.

One of the new ports was a small fishing village called Yokohama. The shogunate packed it with souvenir shops, restaurants, theatres, residential bungalows and brothels, hoping that if foreigners found all they needed in this one place they would be less likely to stray beyond it and cause trouble. The plan worked: Yokohama soon became synonymous both with thriving international trade and with the eccentricities of expat life. One English observer noted that Yokohama seemed to attract the 'scum of Europe'. Another complained of fights breaking out in the middle of the night and firearms being discharged seemingly at random. Yokohama also became a magnet for curious locals looking to try foreign fashions, music and cuisine, from French bread to champagne. In 1864, they were even treated to the sight of a visiting circus, although some of the animals died in the heat. An ice enclosure was hurriedly constructed to keep the survivors cool.

Relationships between Japanese and expats in Yokohama were generally cordial but sometimes became strained. The porcelain, lacquerware, bronzes and ivories found in the souvenir shops were often of poor quality, made for foreigners who were not expected to understand what they were looking at. Some did understand, and resented being taken for fools. Foreign merchants dealing with customs officials meanwhile found that the wheels of Tokugawa bureaucracy turned slowly, and sometimes fell off. They also suffered at the hands of the occasional dishonest Japanese merchant, peddling poor-quality raw silk or tea that was markedly inferior to the tasting sample provided to his unwitting client. These sorts of incidents inflamed westerners' sense of superiority. As an Irish doctor working in Yokohama put it: 'We may disguise it as we like [but] we are a set of tyrants from the moment we set foot on Eastern soil.' For Japanese who were already angry at the terms of what became known as the 'unequal treaties', enmity – sometimes spilling over into violence – in the treaty ports offered compelling evidence that the shogunate was losing control of the country and that something had to be done.

In 1860, the Japanese had a chance to encounter westerners on their home turf. Seventy-seven samurai were sent to America aboard the USS *Powhatan*, forming the first Japanese embassy to the United States. It was an experimental mission in every sense, from the hundreds of thousands of dollars in cash brought along because the intricacies of international credit were not yet understood, to culinary adventures which mostly ended in bitter disappointment. One of the Japanese delegates recalled being presented, at a hotel in San Francisco, with a bowl of 'greasy soup with saltless small fish' bobbing around in it. There was salmon, too, whose preparation seemed to have involved dumping it in some boiling water and then taking it out again. Rice was available, but it was either cooked in butter or mixed with sugar. 'The hardship,' noted Muragaki Norimasa, Lord of Awaji, 'cannot adequately be described with a pen.'

One of the younger members of the delegation was Fukuzawa Yukichi, a man who would one day become known as a great advocate for reform in Japan along western lines. He was fascinated to find that leaders in America had to bid for their own jobs – and even then they could only keep them for a few years at a time. Why, he wanted to know, were the descendants of George Washington not in charge? American dancing appeared no less strange: men and women 'hopping about the room together'. Of more practical use to Japan, concluded the delegates, would be the gas lighting they encountered, advanced surgery under anaesthetic, telescopes and of course weapons. Muragaki noted with disdain the way that military personnel in America were hired for the task rather than being born to it. Put good weapons in the hands of the samurai, he thought, and they might 'destroy America completely'.

A subsequent embassy to Europe, in 1867, was equally instructive. Part of the delegation this time was Shibusawa Eiichi, who like Fukuzawa would one day make a name for himself as a reformer. Shibusawa was not a natural internationalist. In 1861, at the age of twenty-two, he had plotted to set fire to Yokohama, kill some foreigners and allow the shogunate to disappear in the resulting war with the West. Young, activist samurai like him called themselves *shishi* – 'men of high purpose' – and were determined to deal with the foreign threat themselves, having little faith in the shogun and his advisors. But Shibusawa was talked out of his grand plan and ended up in service to the shogunate instead, giving him the chance to see a bit of Europe in 1867: Paris, Basel, Geneva, Brussels, Milan, London and many more places besides. By the time he arrived home again, Shibusawa was convinced of Japan's urgent need for an array of western innovations, from steam engines to financial markets.

Shibusawa might have abandoned his youthful activism, but plenty of his comrades had not. For a great many Japanese, the 1860s were fevered, fearful, unhappy years. The country's abrupt opening-up to global trade had the effect of sending rice prices sky-high, causing serious unrest and inspiring dire predictions of further disasters to come. Foreigners living in places like Yokohama and Edo bore the brunt of Japanese anger, which in a handful of cases escalated to beatings and even murders. There were calls to 'expel the barbarian' combined, among *shishi* in particular, with exhortations to 'revere the Emperor'. The murder of a British merchant named Charles Lennox Richardson by a samurai from Satsuma domain in Kyūshū – despite warnings, Richardson had walked across the path of a Satsuma retinue – brought British, French and Dutch warships into Yokohama in April 1863, forcing the shogunate to make a humiliating indemnity

payment. This was followed in August by an exchange of artillery fire between British ships and the coastal batteries at
Kagoshima, capital of Satsuma domain. Hundreds of homes
were destroyed. The next year, British and French warships
fired on Chōshū domain in retaliation for Chōshū's coastal
batteries being used to attack shipping trying to pass through
the Strait of Shimonoseki.

In both Satsuma and Chōshū, memories remained strong
of being forced to submit to Tokugawa Ieyasu after losing the
Battle of Sekigahara in 1600. Now, a sense of rare and precious opportunity was taking hold, particularly among young
samurai who were dedicated to the cause of restoring the
emperor to power. In 1866, the two domains forged an alliance for mutual protection, and when the shogunate tried
to muster troops to punish them it found that some *daimyō*
were reluctant to contribute men, while the all-important financial backing from Tokugawa's merchant class was slow to
materialise. When the fighting began, the rebel forces proved
to be better armed than those of the shogunate, persuading
the latter to use the death of shogun Iemochi as a pretext
for ordering a retreat. His successor, Yoshinobu, hoped that
a deal with the French to provide military supplies might
yet save the House of Tokugawa. It was not to be. Satsuma,
Chōshū and their allies marched on Kyoto, where with the
help of imperial courtiers they gained control of the teen-
age emperor and pressured Yoshinobu, in November 1867, to
take the momentous step of returning the powers of shogun.

Yoshinobu had been led to believe that he would now lead
a council of *daimyō* serving the emperor. Instead, in January
1868 Satsuma and Chōshū forces – now calling themselves

the 'imperial army' – attacked shogunal forces just outside Kyoto, launching Japan into a civil war that saw a Tokugawa-led coalition pushed steadily northwards up the island of Honshū and across into Ezo. There they established a short-lived republic before succumbing to imperial forces in the summer of 1869. It was the end not just of the Tokugawa shogunate but of almost 700 years of military rule in Japan.

*

1. Deliberative assemblies shall be widely established and all matters decided by public discussion.
2. All classes, high and low, shall be united in vigorously carrying out the administration of affairs of state.
3. The common people, no less than the civil and military officials, shall all be allowed to pursue their own calling so that there may be no discontent.
4. Evil customs of the past shall be broken off and everything based upon the just laws of nature.
5. Knowledge shall be sought throughout the world so as to strengthen the foundation of imperial rule.

Points 4 and 5 on this list might have puzzled Toyotomi Hideyoshi, had he been presented with them. Points 1 to 3, on the other hand, would surely have sent him – in his later years at least – into a murderous frenzy. The idea that everyone in the land ought to do as they please and even have a say in how Japan's affairs were run would have struck him either as completely mad or the work of some foreign enemy determined to sow chaos. And yet this is what the Japanese emperor heard read aloud in the imperial palace in Kyoto in April 1868. Known as the 'Charter Oath' and authored by the leaders of Japan's pro-imperial faction – men like Itō Hirobu-mi and Inoue Kaoru from Chōshū, and Saigō Takamori and Ōkubo Toshimichi from Satsuma – it was intended to serve as a set of basic principles for Japan's future.

The Charter Oath was not an invitation for all and sundry to submit their thoughts on how Japan ought to be governed. It was primarily a call for unity in the face of the enormous challenges facing the country, made by a small group of sam-urai who were only too aware that most Japanese had never heard of them and would not regard them as legitimate rulers if they had. Enterprising use had to be made of the emperor. He was soon installed in Edo Castle, the city around him was renamed Tokyo – 'Eastern Capital' – and a new era name was proclaimed: Meiji. 1868 was 'Meiji 1', and in future the era name would only change when a new emperor ascended the throne. Referred to while he lived by the ancient title *tennō*, 'Heavenly Sovereign', he would bear his reign name in death.

Convening for a while as the Dajōkan, or Great Coun-cil of State – another throwback to the heyday of imperial government – Japan's new leaders launched their country on an astonishingly ambitious programme of reform. Within a few short years, Japan's domains were replaced by prefectures ultimately controlled from Tokyo, and the *daimyō* became part of a new peerage: hereditary, but with little power. Their lavish mansions around Edo Castle – now redesignated the imperial palace – were made to serve as offices for new, western-style government ministries. Samurai status was abolished, and their stipends were eventually converted into one-time gov-ernment bonds. Every household was required to register with the local authority, creating the need for commoners to have surnames. Some possessed them already but had been forbidden during the Tokugawa period from using them in public. Others were forced to make rapid and often rather prosaic choices inspired by their immediate surroundings. These included 'Nishida', meaning 'west field', and 'Tanaka', meaning 'in the middle of the rice paddy'.

New banking, postal and education systems were all rapidly established, and a conscript army was formed from men over the age of twenty: three years of service, followed by four years in the reserves. Land surveys were carried out, and people were awarded the title to their lands, with tax to be paid henceforth in cash as a percentage of the land's value. Old restrictions on how a person dressed, where they went and what jobs they did were all abolished. How much a person made of these freedoms depended, however, on their resources. At the bottom of the Tokugawa social hierarchy had been two groups of outcasts: *hinin* ('non-people'), whose itinerant occupations – often singing or dancing – marked them out from respectable, settled society; and *eta* ('abounding in filth'), so called because their work involved dealing with dead flesh (as butchers, for example, or leather-workers). Both groups were nominally brought into the fold as 'new commoners' but in practice they continued to suffer much of the old stigma.

Amid this whirl of domestic rearrangement, a priority for Japan's ruling clique was to secure the country's borders. The logic of western colonialism appeared to be that any territory not clearly claimed and robustly defended was fair game. That meant rushing to claim Ezo as part of Japan. The territory had, for many centuries, been hunted and fished by the Ainu people, descendants of the ancient Jōmon, with whom Japanese in northern parts of Honshū carried on a limited trade. The island became Hokkaidō ('northern sea circuit') prefecture in 1869. Ten years later, the Ryukyu Islands were annexed as Okinawa prefecture.

Border security, north and south, went hand in hand with an evolving attempt to articulate 'Japanese' standards and values by requiring the people of Hokkaidō and Okinawa prefectures to conform to them. For the Ainu, especially, this was a disaster. Most of their land was taken and given over to mainlander migrants coming in from Honshū. They were required to change their names, cut their hair, abandon much of their culture, adopt Japanese styles of dress, speak the Japanese language and send their children to special 'Native Schools'. All this launched the Ainu into a downward spiral of poverty, alcoholism and abuse at the hands of mainlanders from which it took them more than a century to begin to recover.

The importance of instilling a sense of national belonging and purpose in people across Japan, who until now had identified themselves primarily with their domain or village, was brought home to Japan's leaders by a diplomatic tour of the globe on which they embarked in 1871. One of the aims of the Iwakura Mission, named for the former imperial courtier Iwakura Tomomi, who led it, was to begin the process of revising the unequal treaties. Although it failed in this regard, the mission proved invaluable as a fact-finding expedition, identifying suitable models for the institutions that were required back home. Japan's banking system ended up being based on an American model, and its postal and telegraph services on those of Britain. Medicine was established along German lines, while Tokyo's police force looked to Paris for inspiration.

Beginning in the 1870s, the gap between urban and rural Japan began to widen dramatically. Schools, conscription and altered tax conditions represented important new realities for the majority of Japanese who lived in the countryside, but otherwise life carried on much as before. Residents of Tokyo and Osaka, on the other hand, watched their cities change almost overnight, with fresh styles of building, street lighting, trains, trams and telegraph wires, alongside brand-new forms of work. Not everyone prospered, by any means: migrants in search of work often found themselves penniless and living in slums. And, as a wealthy middle-class took shape across the decades, their prosperity visible in their enjoyment of new opportunities for shopping and entertainment, the sense would begin to build among poorer rural folk that their labour was funding alien lifestyles and their interests were being ignored. The implications of such sentiments for Japan's politics, and its place in the world, would be grave.

Japan's encounter with the West in the second half of the 1800s did not run all one way. Artists like Kawanabe Kyōsai found themselves fielding requests, in the 1870s and 1880s, from western counterparts seeking tuition. Born in 1831, Kyōsai had studied as a boy with Utagawa Kuniyoshi, a late master of the *ukiyo-e* woodblock print who was best known for depicting samurai heroes caught up in ghostly, gory nightmares. *Takiyasha the Witch and the Skeleton Spectre* (c. 1844) was one of Utagawa's finest: a triptych showing Princess Takiyasha, daughter of a tenth-century provincial nobleman, summoning a great skeleton to intimidate a visiting imperial official named Mitsukuni. Utagawa's near-contemporaries had included Katsushika Hokusai (1760–1849) and Andō Hiroshige (1797–1858), both of whom were influenced by western artistic techniques and materials making their way into Japan via the Dutch at Nagasaki. Hokusai's famous *Great Wave off Kanagawa* would have struck Japanese viewers as thoroughly western in its use of perspective. It was made using a pigment imported from Holland known as 'Prussian blue'.

Utagawa, Hokusai and Hiroshige all passed away before the imperial restoration and political revolution of the late 1860s and 1870s. But Kyōsai lived to see the drama unfold. His *Fashionable Picture of the Great Frog Battle* (1864) depicted violence breaking out in a lily pond between groups of frogs armed with water-cannon and bulrush spears. Crests adorning the curtains of each encampment reveal this to be a clan allied to the Tokugawa clashing with pro-imperial Chōshū domain. Other works by Kyōsai satirised the great experiments in fashion and food that were a feature of the 1860s and 1870s, from western suit jackets worn over kimono to the return of beef – often marinaded in miso or soy sauce – to a country where Buddhist influence had rendered it taboo for more than a thousand years. One of his paintings shows a skeleton wearing a western-style top hat and samurai sword, playing the shamisen while a tiny monster dances jigs in the foreground. Another, *School for Spooks* (*Bakebake gakkō*), features the offspring of demons and water-spirits sitting in a new, western-style school, complete with benches, desks, boards and besuited masters.

Somewhat to the disappointment of Japan's new leaders, who hoped to show their country in the most sophisticated light possible, western artists and art-lovers homed in on the popular traditions of comic sketches and *ukiyo-e* art that Kyōsai represented. Vincent Van Gogh and Claude Monet were among the more prominent admirers of these styles, collecting prints and borrowing Japanese techniques for their work. Some, like the Australian-born painter Mortimer Menpes, had the chance to go to Japan and watch artists like Kyōsai at work. Menpes encountered Kyōsai in 1887 at an event known as a *shogakai*: a mass gathering of artists and calligraphers held in a large restaurant, where paying guests could call out a request and have a piece dashed off spontaneously in response. Menpes later recalled that it was only after drinking a great deal of *sake* that Kyōsai, by this point in his mid-fifties, had been persuaded to take part:

> He looked like a god as he knelt there, gripping his brush and staring at the silk – he was seeing his picture. He executed a flight of crows, a masterpiece . . . Proudly drawing himself up to his full height, quivering in every limb, he threw down his brush, skidded the silk along the floor to the spectators, and saying 'That is Kyōsai', left the house.

Another western admirer of Kyōsai was the British architect Josiah Conder, who studied painting under him while designing some of Tokyo's new buildings. These included the Rokumeikan, 'Deer-Cry Hall', which was intended as a place where Japanese and foreign elites might socialise together. Men like Itō Hirobumi, who had studied for a short time at University College London, were convinced that culture and character would matter in Japan's global affairs. They hoped, ideally, to see Japan represented abroad by its more traditional and respectable forms of art including ceramics, painting styles from the Heian and Muromachi periods, metalwork and religious statuary. Institutions were set up to champion these favoured forms, including the Tokyo National Museum (1872) and the Tokyo School of Fine Arts (1887). Efforts were meanwhile made to reinvent Nō and *kabuki* as Japan's answers to European theatre and opera.

For conservative newspaper commentators in Japan, these attempts at cultural diplomacy appeared to be weighted heavily in favour of naïve enthusiasm for all things western. Conder's Rokumeikan became a popular target: a place where Japanese politicians and diplomats indulged in the ignominious imitation of western life – cocktails and ballroom dancing – while westerners laughed at them behind their backs. From the mid-1880s, a conservative backlash gathered pace, just as the future shape of Japanese society and politics was being hammered out. Education reforms replaced the western textbooks that had been hurriedly put to use in the 1870s with new Japanese ones, some of which held up Tokugawa Ieyasu as an enduring ethical model for the country's youth. An Imperial Rescript on Education in 1890, sent out to every school in the land alongside a portrait of the emperor, emphasised Confucian values of filial respect for parents, harmonious marriages, benevolent treatment of others and modesty and moderation in one's manner of living. It also reflected the seamless blending of the ancient and the modern that was becoming the hallmark of Meiji-era reforms, referencing the 'Imperial Ancestors' while requiring people, 'should emergency arise', to 'offer yourselves courageously to the State'.

The most important document of the age was the Constitution of the Empire of Japan, proclaimed in February 1889. It was the culmination of twenty years of political battles over how the principles of the Charter Oath of 1868 should be put into practice. Some had dared to hope, on the basis of the first of the five principles – 'Deliberative assemblies shall be widely established and all matters decided by public discussion' – that British- or French-style democracy might be coming to Japan. A Freedom and People's Rights movement had emerged to press for this outcome, inspired by an influx into Japan of texts on western history and political philosophy. Japan's first political parties had been formed, too: Jiyūtō (Freedom Party) and Rikken Kaishintō (Constitutional Progressive Party).

But the small group of coup leaders who continued to steer Japan's course in the 1880s had no intention of ceding power. Their ardour for 'public discussion' cooled to the point where a number of Freedom and People's Rights meetings were broken up by the police, forcing others to be held on barges in the middle of lakes. As for 'deliberative assemblies', their purpose was ideally twofold: to serve as a channel of communication from Japan's leaders to the population at large (and not the other way around), and to allow those who sought political influence to feel important without actually enjoying any real authority.

Japan's new constitution reflected these sentiments, placing the emperor at the head of the armed forces and in charge of all appointments to a new cabinet, judiciary and House of Peers. Japan gained an elected lower house, the House of Representatives. But only around 5 per cent of the adult male population were eligible to vote, based on age (twenty-five and over) and the amount of tax they paid, and it enjoyed very little power. That lay with the cabinet and the ministries they controlled. The former was composed chiefly of the coup leaders of 1868 along with their protégés, with Itō Hirobumi serving as Japan's first prime minister. The ministries, meanwhile, were staffed by career bureaucrats who had been educated for the most part at the new Tokyo University and who regarded themselves as 'shepherds of the people', as one put it. Their job was to anticipate Japan's evolving needs as it modernised, to formulate policies to address those needs and to ensure – via moral suasion of the sort found in Tokugawa-era edicts – that the public followed along as required.

The Meiji Civil Code, issued in 1898, was similarly conservative in nature. The basic social and legal unit in Japan was to be the household, or *ie*, rather than the individual. At the head of the household was the father, who passed the role on to his son. Women were, in legal terms, second-class citizens: barred from testifying in court or bringing legal proceedings of their own. Women were also forbidden, from 1890 onwards, from taking part in politics. The ideal middle-class woman was instead a 'Good Wife and Wise Mother'. In an era when the physical and psychological condition of Japan's workforce and armed forces was regarded as integral to the country's fortunes, this was a critically important role.

Those armed forces became the focal point of national pride in 1894–5, when tensions with China over influence on the Korean Peninsula turned into war and Japan's new army and navy – based on Prussian and British models, respectively – were sent into action. They chased the Chinese out of Korea, invaded Manchuria and seized parts of the strategically important Liaodong Peninsula on Manchuria's southern tip. They even began to threaten Beijing, at which point the Chinese sued for peace. Newspaper readers in Japan were delighted to learn that under the Treaty of Shimonoseki, which brought the war to an end, Japan would take control of Taiwan and the Liaodong Peninsula and would receive an indemnity payment of 200 million taels of silver (the equivalent of around $9 billion dollars in today's money). Before long, however, those same newspapers carried news of an intervention by Russia, France and Germany, made – as they rather piously put it – for the 'peace of Asia' and requiring Japan to return the Liaodong Peninsula to Chinese control. It was a harsh lesson in global realpolitik, made worse in 1898 when Russia won itself a long-term lease of that same peninsula, allowing the Russians to establish a potentially threatening warm-water naval base at Port Arthur.

Russo-Japanese relations soured from here, and in 1904 the Japanese launched a surprise attack on their far larger neighbour. Admiral Tōgō Heihachirō became a national hero when the Japanese navy managed to sink almost the entire Russian Baltic fleet after its epic journey around the world to join the fray. The British, with whom the Japanese had entered into an anti-Russian alliance in 1902, gifted Tōgō a lock of Admiral Lord Nelson's hair by way of congratulation. After months of exceptionally bloody fighting, particularly on the Liaodong Peninsula, Japan's armed forces once again proved their worth. It was a far more significant victory than Japan's earlier one over China because it was the first time in the modern era that an Asian power had vanquished a European one. Anti-colonial nationalists celebrated a turning-point moment. India's future prime minister, Jawaharlal Nehru, described it as a 'great pick-me-up for Asia'.

Under the Treaty of Portsmouth brokered by US President Theodore Roosevelt, Japan regained control of the Liaodong Peninsula, benefiting from the work that the Russians had done there to lay railway track and develop mines. Japan's special interest in the Korean Peninsula was meanwhile recognised, opening the way for the annexation of Korea in 1910. But 100,000 men died in the Japan–Russia conflict on the Japanese side alone, and for all that popular domestic sentiment in favour of the conflict remained strong, there was an undercurrent of misgiving and even dissent that could not be ignored. This was memorably expressed by the young poet Yosano Akiko in a protest poem addressed to her brother, who was among the soldiers laying siege to Port Arthur. Yosano seemed to marshal every government-sponsored value she could think of to oppose the conflict. Their parents had not raised them 'to kill and die'. They were a merchant family with no interest in what happened at Port Arthur. Surely the emperor could not condone all this senseless waste of life:

> His Majesty the Emperor
> Goes not himself into the battle.
> Could he, with such deeply noble heart,
> Think it an honour for men
> To spill one another's blood
> And die like beasts?

Few of Japan's newspaper editors had much sympathy for the likes of Yosano Akiko. Mainstream Japanese society, whose attitudes and values they helped to shape, largely supported the government in seeking to build Japan's prosperity at home and its stature abroad and were prepared to play their allocated parts: tilling fields, serving in the army, raising children or taking jobs in the range of privately run industries on which so much of Japan's wealth now depended. When the Meiji emperor passed away in the summer of 1912, people kneeled and wept at the palace gates.

And yet the energies and aspirations unleashed across the 1850s, 1860s and 1870s, fuelled by the rapid circulation of new ideas about how people might live, societies might be organised and countries might be run, were such that for all Japan's achievements across the lifespan of the Meiji emperor, this was not a country entirely at ease with itself. There were plenty of women of Yosano Akiko's generation who wanted to write, work or play a role in the country's politics. Those who did have jobs, notably the young women and girls who laboured long hours for little pay in industries like silk-reeling, wanted more humane conditions of work – free of beatings and the risk of tuberculosis. Japan was home to socialists and anarchists, too, and even would-be regicides: in 1910, police were tipped off about a plot to assassinate the emperor. Out in the countryside, the pain of having to pay fixed taxes regardless of the quality of that year's harvest or the vicissitudes of an economy now tethered to global trade and prices occasionally erupted into violent protest. Nor had the samurai been willing to go quietly: 20,000 of them from south-western Japan had tried to march on Tokyo in 1876, only to be cut down by the carbines and artillery of the new conscript army.

In colonised Korea, meanwhile, Japan was creating for itself a legacy of lasting bitterness. Japanese farmers were awarded large tracts of land, turning their Korean counterparts into tenants overnight. Anthropologists and archaeologists were sent across to the peninsula, too, there to trace the contours of a culture deemed inferior to Japan while funnelling some of the most precious finds back into Japanese museums and private collections. Japan's 'civilising mission' in Korea included the establishment of modern institutions and infrastructure, from which Japanese businessmen like Shibusawa profited immensely. It centred, however, on education. A Japanese school system was put in place, teaching Japanese moral and political values alongside Korean culture and history. The balance shifted decisively in favour of Japanese language, culture and loyalty to the emperor from the late 1930s onwards, as Japan dragged Korea with it through its dark valley.

Even in the section of society that seemed to have gained the most in the new Japan, middle-class urban men, there was disquiet in the early 1910s. Sōseki Natsume novel *Kokoro* (*The Heart of Things*, 1914), depicted a generation of young men caught between an old set of values that was passing away with their parents and a new world whose choices and opportunities were capable of inspiring a deep loneliness and uncertainty of purpose. Such was the cultural impact, in Japan, of the opening of its doors to the West in the 1850s, that these and other challenges often came to be framed in terms of Japanese versus western ways of doing things.

There was no set definition of 'Japanese', and Natsume Sōseki was among those to satirise the idea of a 'Japanese spirit':

> Admiral Tōgō possesses the Japanese spirit, and the local fishmonger has it as well. Swindlers and murderers also have the Japanese spirit. Since it is a spirit it is always blurry

and fuzzy; there is no one in Japan who hasn't had it on the tip of his tongue, but there's no one who has actually seen it.

Still, one of the most important and least predictable legacies of the coup leaders of 1868 was their attempt to instil in the population a sense of 'Japaneseness' as something privileged and precious, ancient and modern, at once path-breaking – witness the country's rapid and successful modernisation – and vulnerable, given the overwhelming rapacity of the major western powers.

In centuries past, unity in Japan had eventually fallen victim to regional identities and interests: the imperial court lost out to provincial warrior families; the Kamakura and Ashikaga shogunates were undermined by employees who turned their areas of operation into personal fiefdoms; the Tokugawa shogunate was felled by a coalition of south-western samurai with long memories. The Meiji settlement, which looked so secure in 1912, would soon face a different challenge altogether: the steady poisoning of the very idea of unity, as an ever-greater range of ideas was dismissed as 'un-Japanese' and the interests of the nation were invoked in steering a perilous political course both at home and abroad.

# CHAPTER 8

# The Dark Valley

Following victories over China in 1895 and Russia in 1905, the outbreak of the Great War in 1914 once again gave Japan the chance to stand tall on the world stage. Its alliance with Great Britain did not oblige Japan to enter the conflict, but by declaring war on Germany on 23 August, Japan's leaders gave themselves the opportunity to make some useful territorial gains. Troops occupied German colonies and bases in the Asia-Pacific region. These included concessions on China's Shandong Peninsula, home to the German East Asiatic Squadron, alongside the Mariana, Caroline and Marshall Islands. Japan was now a (very modest) Pacific power.

Japan also supplied medical teams to Europe via the Japanese Red Cross and sent escort vessels to the Indian Ocean and the Mediterranean. But some of the goodwill thus earned was squandered by Japan's 'Twenty-One Demands' on China in 1915. These included obliging China to accept Japanese advisors to help run its finances and police forces and allowing Japan to establish railways, temples, mining operations and schools on its territory. Had the demands been accepted in full, Japan would have enjoyed extraordinary control over China's political and economic affairs. The United States in particular, regarding itself as a friend of China, was angered by what even senior politicians in Japan regarded as a foolish initiative.

When the time came to negotiate a postwar peace, Japan enjoyed a seat at the top table, as one of five 'Principal Allied and Associated Powers'. And yet by the time the Treaty of Versailles came to be signed, in the opulent Hall of Mirrors at the Palace of Versailles in June 1919, it was regarded as the achievement of the 'Big Four': US President Woodrow Wilson alongside the prime ministers of Britain, France and Italy. One of the problems for Japan was its underpowered negotiating team. Where the other major powers sent senior political leaders to Paris – presidents, prime ministers, foreign ministers – Japan was represented by genial old diplomats like Baron Makino Nobuaki: good company, as far as their western counterparts were concerned, but second-tier statesmen who lacked the skills or executive authority required to negotiate at a high level and swift tempo. They also struggled to articulate themselves forcefully in English, prone instead to the quiet observation of proceedings.

The biggest disappointment of the Paris Peace Conference, from Japan's point of view, was the failure to have a racial equality clause inserted into the Covenant of the League of Nations. Chinese and Japanese migrants to the United States, Australia, Canada and New Zealand over recent decades had discovered that they were not always welcomed with open arms. Alongside talk of a 'yellow peril' and 'filthy hordes' ran legislation aimed at limiting migration from East Asia. A case in point was the California Alien Land Law of 1913, under which people who were ineligible for citizenship were forbidden from owning agricultural land. The law was regarded as being aimed squarely at Japanese migrants, and the Japanese government protested against it at the time.

The Japanese government in Tokyo was not primarily concerned about the feelings or prospects of the largely poor rural families who left Japan in hopes of better lives abroad. Nor was it seeking to strike a blow against racism in all its forms: Japan's emergence as a regional power in Asia was attended and even underpinned by racial antipathy and discrimination towards the people of China and Korea, and there was little evidence of Japan being keen to champion African political aspirations. The desire for a racial equality clause had more to do with fears about what the League of Nations might mean for Japan's status in Asia and the Pacific. It seemed all too likely that, despite the lofty Wilsonian rhetoric floating around the negotiations in Paris, the new League would end up serving as a vehicle for white western powers to continue the pursuit of their own interests around the world. A proposal for a racial equality clause was duly put forward as an amendment to Article 21 on religious freedom:

> The equality of nations being a basic principle of the League of Nations, the High Contracting Parties agree to accord as soon as possible to all alien nationals of all states, members of the League, equal and just treatment in every respect making no distinction, either in law or in fact, on account of their race or nationality.

Stiff resistance from Australia, whose delegates worried about the potential of such a clause to be taken as implying support for unrestricted immigration, led to a watering-down of the proposal. Even then, it failed, partly because the Americans were less committed to the idea than they had led the Japanese to believe. The reaction back home in Japan was one of outrage, since the proposal had become a litmus test both of Japan's bargaining strength abroad and the quality of the country's diplomats. Those at the more hawkish end of the Japanese establishment – the sort who had advocated for the demands made on China in 1915 – concluded that diplomats were, by their nature, too fond of foreigners to be capable of acting robustly in Japan's interests.

This idea, that perfidious westerners and spineless Japanese diplomats were conspiring to thwart Japan's global ambitions, became an influential theme across the 1920s. Internationalists in Japan, of whom there were many, hoped that this would be a decade of peaceful co-operation after the carnage of the Great War. By contrast, members of the Japanese armed forces who were too young to recall a time when Japan had been weak and vulnerable believed that Japan ought to be preparing for a future conflict with the United States, Russia or both. Strategists in the United States were thinking in much the same way. The 1920s saw the first drafts produced of 'War Plan Orange': a strategy for war against Japan, launched primarily from American naval bases in Hawaii, Guam and the Philippines.

At home, the period between the end of the Russo-Japanese War in 1905 and the death of the Taishō emperor in 1926 came to be remembered as the high point of Japan's democratic experiment. In 1918, Hara Kei became the first man to rise through the ranks of a political party to become prime minister, ending a trend for the post to be passed around members of the country's ruling clique – Itō Hirobumi, for example, had been appointed to the role no fewer than four times during his long career. Across the 1920s, most of the top jobs in government were filled by elected politicians, a shift made all the more radical by the fact that from 1925 the franchise was expanded to include all men over the age of twenty-five regardless of income level. Japan's political parties began to attract civil servants and businessmen into their ranks as never before: a sure sign that the limited role originally envisaged for the lower house of the Diet (parliament) was giving way to something more substantial.

For anyone with a bit of money to spend, cities like Tokyo and Osaka now had a great deal to offer: French cinema, American jazz, comedy clubs, food from all over the world, lavish department-store shopping and highly efficient transport networks. The ban on women's participation in politics was lifted in 1922, and although women did not yet have the vote, writers like Yosano Akiko and Hiratsuka Raichō began to give voice via magazines like *Seitō* (*Blue Stocking*) to women who wanted more from life than – in Hiratsuka's words – being 'their husbands' slaves during the daytime and their prostitutes at night'. Bustling city life was celebrated in popular song, and so many rural Japanese were drawn to the imagined opportunities of life in Tokyo that the city doubled in size within a generation, reaching 4 million people by 1923.

Then disaster struck. Residents of Tokyo and Yokohama were used to the sensation of the ground beneath them shaking now and again. This part of Japan, the Kanto Plain, lay at the meeting point of four tectonic plates. You only needed to worry if the shaking failed to stop, or became more severe.

Shortly before noon on 1 September 1923, a series of side-to-side tremors began, continued longer than was usual and then gave way to violent vertical convulsions so powerful that they were felt as far away as Spain and California. Buildings began to collapse, gas pipes ruptured and charcoal fires being used to prepare lunch overturned, setting fire to homes that in this era were still mostly built from wood and paper.

As hot air was channelled down narrow streets, whirling firestorms engulfed entire neighbourhoods. Tokyo's river and canal bridges became crammed with people trying to flee the city with their possessions, as the smoke thickened around them and rumours began to circulate that Mount Fuji was about to erupt. Only after days of chaos and mounting desperation were roads and railways cleared and repaired so that food and medical supplies could reach the city over land and warships and merchant vessels bringing in aid by sea could be unloaded. By that time, more than 100,000 people were dead and over half of Tokyo's population was homeless.

There were those in the aftermath of the Great Kantō Earthquake who regarded it as divine punishment visited on a decadent city too much in love with money and frivolous forms of entertainment. This was a minority view, but in a country whose media and intellectuals had become used to reflecting on rapid social change, the earthquake inspired agonised questioning. Why did Tokyo have so many slums, rife with tuberculosis and cholera? Was the city's population of young independent women, working in offices and cafés and spending their money on the latest French or American fashions, a sign of progress or of declining morality? Why had rumours spread so readily during the earthquake that the city's Korean residents were rising up – looting, killing and poisoning wells? And how was it possible that thousands of Koreans had been murdered in cold blood – were they really all the victims of criminals, opportunists and corrupt police, rather than of ordinary people who had been overtaken by extraordinary hatred?

Questions and worries like these prompted Japan's prime minister and his cabinet to look at ways in which moral education in schools could be improved. Boy Scouts were sent into the ruins of Tokyo and Yokohama to collect tales of heroism and self-sacrifice. Meanwhile, the cities were gradually rebuilt, with wider, paved roads, upgraded bridges and water systems, and new parks complete with playgrounds and baseball diamonds. Public dining halls and baths were built to support poorer residents.

At first, life in Tokyo felt as though it were returning to normal. Commerce carried on as before, people flooded back and the city's transport system was expanded with the opening of the circular Yamanote Line in 1925. Radio came to Japan the same year, and people flocked to the cinema to enjoy some of the country's first samurai films. And yet, as the 1920s wore on, two themes in modern Japanese life that dated back at least as far as the 1860s began to make their way to the fore: population management and the romance of the past.

The coup leaders of 1868 had seen it as their priority to manage the population for the sake of Japanese security in a dangerous world. A spate of riots in the summer of 1918 over high rice prices brought home to the country's politicians the speed with which economic problems could give rise to unrest – serious enough, in this case, to require bringing in troops – and potentially help the spread of radical left-wing ideologies. These worries intensified over the course of the 1920s as industrialisation turned Japan into a mass society, with all the risk that carried of large labour forces concentrated in urban areas like Yokohama and Kobe and agitating for better wages and working conditions.

With this in mind, the granting of universal male suffrage in 1925 was accompanied by the passing of a draconian new Peace Preservation Law aimed at the suppression of socialists and communists. People were now forbidden from expressing opposition towards Japan's political arrangements or to the principle of private ownership. And much was made of the concept of *kokutai*: the state conceived as a 'national body', an organic whole with the emperor at its head. Offences against the *kokutai* were punishable by lengthy prison sentences, and after 1928 could attract the death penalty. Even before this, a great many socialists and communists had suffered a de facto death penalty, passing away in the custody of the Special Higher Police (Tokkō), formed in the aftermath of the assassination plot against the Meiji emperor in 1910.

Even moderate thinkers in Japan were wedded to the idea that the challenges of a modern mass society ought to be met by elite-led conciliation rather than competition and social strife. The constitutional theorist Yoshino Sakuzō suggested that rather than western-style government *by* the people, Japan ought to aim for government *for* the people (*minponshugi*). In other words, the country should be run in the people's interests by suitably qualified civil servants, of whom there were no fewer than 1.3 million in Japan in 1928: the equivalent of 5 per cent of everyone in work. Meanwhile, the favoured means of dealing with labour unrest was for the police to pick off the more implacable elements while civil servants helped to mediate between workers making moderate demands and large employers like Mitsubishi.

Japan's feminists found that their political aspirations were treated in a similar way. Demands for enfranchisement were consistently blocked, but civil servants in Tokyo and around the country were happy to enlist them in public information campaigns promoting health, hygiene, frugality and the saving of money for a rainy day. Progressive outliers like Yosano Akiko and Hiratsuka Raichō aside, women were thought to be naturally conservative, particularly on social questions, making them valuable allies in the struggle against left-wing ideologies.

Those ideologies were often described as 'un-Japanese': a charge increasingly levelled at western culture in general. Negative views of the West had quite a pedigree by this point. In the Tokugawa era, the Dutch had been regarded as silly and barbarous – given to wearing clogs, it was said, because their feet resembled those of dogs, with heels that did not touch the ground. In the early Meiji era, a prominent Confucian scholar named Motoda Eifu, tutor to the emperor no less, charged that western values amounted to no more than 'fact-gathering and technique'. Debates about western political philosophies around the same time featured arguments over whether the concept of 'freedom' ought to be regarded positively, in terms of self-mastery, or negatively, as self-centredness run riot.

Writers like Tanizaki Junichirō helped to feed a nostalgia for the Japanese past. In the aftermath of the earthquake, he relocated from Yokohama – where his home had been destroyed – to Kyoto, shifting at the same time from an interest in all that was western and modern in Japanese life to an exploration of Japanese aesthetics. He went on to make the famous claim that westerners live in a banal world of simple opposites, as though in a room where a single light bulb is either on or off. Japanese, by contrast, experience life as though by candlelight: subtle, shifting and beautiful.

Economic problems served to compound the sense that the population must be carefully managed and that Japan's modern encounter with the West was turning sour. Inflation caused by rapid growth during the Great War was never fully brought under control, and Japan found itself less competitive than before on international markets. The countryside was hit especially hard by the global depression after 1929, as silk prices collapsed.

Neither of Japan's two main political parties enjoyed the kind of grassroots membership that would allow them effectively to express some of the anger that all this hardship caused. The conservative Seiyūkai (Friends of Constitutional Government) had strong ties to landlords, big business, the civil service and the military. Minseitō (Constitutional People's Party) was more liberal in its inclinations: universal male suffrage had been one of its policies, as was the Tenancy Conciliation Law, passed in 1924 with the aim of helping tenant farmers to negotiate rent levels with landlords when times were tough. But it, too, was primarily dependent on interest-group support, in particular businesses and liberal-minded bureaucrats.

The result was a lack of sympathy for civilian politicians among ordinary Japanese. Instead, in a country where three-quarters of politically active adults in 1930 had been born in the countryside and almost all adult men had experience of military service, there was only one Japanese institution that could plausibly claim to embody the highest values of selflessness and service: the armed forces.

Liberal internationalists in Japan became used, across the 1920s and early 1930s, to disappointment. The failure to have a racial equality clause included in the Covenant of the League of Nations was followed, in 1924, by America's passing of a Japanese Exclusion Act. No one who was ineligible for citizenship in the US would now be allowed to enter the country as an immigrant – a category into which a Supreme Court ruling two years earlier had explicitly placed all Japanese people. International arms control agreements, too, appeared to go against Japan. In 1921, Britain, the United States and Japan agreed the Washington Naval Treaty, setting a 5:5:3 tonnage ratio for battleships and aircraft carriers. Diplomats like Shidehara Kijūrō regarded this ratio as sufficient for Japan's needs in East Asia and the Pacific. Critics thought that kind of attitude complacent and even naïve. So-called 'international co-operation' struck them as little more than the latest packaging devised by western powers to protect their hegemony.

Added to this, for those who worried about Japan's security, was the growing presence of the Soviet Union in north-east Asia and the steady success of China's nationalists, under Chiang Kai-shek and his Kuomintang party, in reunifying China. The London Naval Treaty of 1930, which built on the achievements of the Washington treaty almost a decade earlier, was regarded by its opponents as threatening to undermine Japan's security still further. One young ultranationalist took matters into his own hands in November that year by shooting and seriously injuring Prime Minister Hamaguchi Osachi at Tokyo Station.

From this point on, the ultra-nationalist right was far more of a threat than the left to stability in Japan. Officers in the Kwantung Army, whose job it was to look after security on the Liaodong Peninsula in Manchuria, decided to engineer a conflict with local Chinese troops that would allow the army to shore up its position in the area. One of the plotters was Lieutenant Ishiwara Kanji, a convert to Nichiren Buddhism who interpreted Nichiren's thirteenth-century prophecies about Japan's downfall as a warning that the long-awaited conflict with the United States was on its way. The plot was spectacularly successful: by setting off a small explosion on some railway track just outside Mukden in September 1931, and arranging for some bodies dressed in Chinese military uniform to be discovered at the scene, the Kwantung Army was able to claim sabotage and go on the offensive against Chinese troops stationed nearby.

As fighting spread across Manchuria, the government in Tokyo was faced with an army unit that had gone rogue, and domestic newspapers that were determined to cheer it on and cast the Chinese as the aggressors. Prime Minister Wakatsuki Reijirō, successor to the injured Hamaguchi, was forced to resign along with his entire cabinet. By March 1932, Manchuria was entirely in the hands of the Kwantung Army. The state of 'Manchukuo' was declared, with the last emperor of China, Puyi, serving as its puppet ruler.

A few weeks later, on Sunday 15 May 1932, Wakatsuki's replacement as prime minister, Inukai Tsuyoshi, was at home expecting a visit from Charlie Chaplin when a group of young, ultra-nationalist naval officers burst into his home and shot him dead. They had hoped to kill Chaplin, too, thus provoking a conflict with the United States. Elsewhere in Tokyo, other activists – a mixture of military men and farmers – were busy attacking banks, electric power stations and the police head-quarters, seeking 'in the name of the Emperor' to rid Japan of sell-out civilian political elites and businessmen. Amid what one foreign journalist called 'government by assassination', civilian politicians turned to senior military figures to help stabilise the country, inviting them to join the cabinet.

Japan's international relationships meanwhile soured dramatically over Manchuria. A motion censuring Japan over its actions there and recommending that it withdraw its troops was adopted by the League of Nations in February 1933 by forty-two votes to one, with only Japan voting against. The head of Japan's delegation, Matsuoka Yōsuke, had been part of the Paris Peace Conference delegation back in 1919 and had seen at first hand the ignominious failure of Japanese diplomacy when its demand for a racial equality clause was denied. He now made a final impassioned speech declaring that Japan had done its best to support the League but would not tolerate interference with its affairs in Manchuria. Announcing that Japan was leaving the League, he strode out of the hall to a combination of hissing and applause, calling over his shoulder as he went: 'We are not coming back!'

In the short term, Japan's international isolation helped its economy to rebound from the recent depression. A great deal of money was spent on building up the country's industrial and military strength, much of it flowing into the coffers of the *zaibatsu*: conglomerates like Mitsubishi and Mitsui, which were active across a wide range of industries and benefited from impeccable political and civil service connections – sometimes extending to intermarriage between family members. These were high times, too, for Japan's civil servants, as the state gained ever-greater control of the economy, in particular key industries like coal, iron, steel, electricity generation, shipbuilding and automobile and aircraft manufacturing.

Improved economic fortunes did little to turn down the political temperature in Japan. The ultra-nationalist right continued to garner support among a younger generation of military personnel, particularly in the army, alongside rural Japanese who were inclined to blame their suffering in recent years on distant urbanites with foreign tastes and allegiances. On 26 February 1936, young officers led more than a thousand soldiers in a coup attempt, taking over the Diet building in Tokyo alongside a number of government buildings. It took intervention by a rival army faction, the sending of forty navy ships into Tokyo Bay and a personal expression of displeasure by the emperor himself to restore order.

Fraught politics at home narrowed Japan's options abroad. When fighting briefly broke out on 7 July 1937 between Chinese troops and Japanese counterparts stationed in the area of the Marco Polo bridge just outside Beijing, it ought to have been possible to prevent escalation. Neither side stood much to gain from all-out war. But Chiang Kai-shek and the Japanese Prime Minister Konoe Fumimarō were both under pressure from their domestic audiences to show strength, and in the end it proved impossible to contain the crisis. Japanese troops overran Beijing and then Shanghai, before entering the Kuomintang capital Nanjing at the end of 1937 and unleashing extraordinary carnage on the civilian population there, leading to many tens of thousands of deaths.

By the end of 1938, 850,000 Japanese troops had been committed to the fight in China, and there was little sign of a resolution to the conflict. The government continued to try to tighten its control of the economy, battling business leaders who were happy to take government contracts but who baulked at having their access to resources and their production programmes dictated to them by civil servants. In need of a grand strategy to make sense of all this, Konoe's government announced the intention, in the summer of 1940, of creating a Greater East Asia Co-Prosperity Sphere (GEAPS). A bloc of countries, including Japan, China, Manchukuo and parts of South-East Asia, would co-operate in ridding the region of western colonial power.

This grand plan for Asia was soon yoked to the war in Europe. Back in November 1936, Japan and Germany had signed an Anti-Comintern Pact, aimed squarely at the Soviet Union. Now, in September 1940, Japan agreed a defensive alliance with Germany and Italy via a Tripartite Pact, directed mainly at the United States. Japan never fully embraced fascist ideology. Its Meiji-era institutions remained in place, albeit serving an increasingly authoritarian statism as the 1930s wore on. Nevertheless, sides had now been chosen and battle lines drawn. The apocalyptic conflict about which Ishiwara Kanji had long fantasised appeared, at last, to be on its way.

*

As Japan's estrangement from its erstwhile western allies deepened across the 1930s, efforts were made to explain this trend of events to the population and to persuade them of the necessity for sacrifices: family members conscripted, freedoms curtailed and food rationed. In 1937, a document was produced and sent out to schools called the *Kokutai No Hongi* (*Fundamentals of Our National Polity*). Its aim was to explain current events within the grand sweep of history:

> The various ideological and social evils of present-day Japan are the result of ignoring the fundamental and running after the trivial, of lack of judgment, and a failure to digest things thoroughly; and this is due to the fact that since the days of *Meiji* so many aspects of European and American culture, systems and learning have been imported . . . We [Imperial] subjects are intrinsically quite different from the so-called citizens of the Occidental countries.

The *Kokutai no Hongi* went on to explain those differences. Whereas in the West a nation was little more than a 'conglomeration of separate individuals independent of each other', the relationship in Japan between emperor and subject ran so deep that the perfection of the latter's existence lay in 'receiv[ing] the Emperor's great august Will as one's own'. This was the meaning of *kokutai*: Japan as a single 'national body'. Any other kind of selfhood was mere 'corruption of the spirit'.

In case this felt a little abstract to children and parents reading the *Kokutai no Hongi*, the text went on to declare that 'Our country is a great family nation, and the Imperial Household is the head family of the subjects and the nucleus of national life.' Family values and filial piety, alongside *bushidō*, understood as 'a sense of obligation [which] binds master and servant', were the only way for a country truly to succeed. Societies premised on individualism were destined to fail through endless 'clashes' and 'class wars'.

One ought not to mistake propaganda, which the *Kokutai no Hongi* undoubtedly was, for reliable information about the outlook of Japan's leaders in the late 1930s and early 1940s. But somewhere in the calculations of men like prime minister Konoe Fumimarō was the idea that the Chinese and Americans, in their differing ways, were made of lesser stuff than the Japanese. Chinese nationalism, thought Konoe, was not robust enough to withstand an all-out war with Japan – people's hearts, in the end, would not be in it. When it came to the United States, Japanese policy-makers seem to have operated with some combination of belief and hope in the idea that the American public would not support the horrors of another major war.

Running alongside such calculations was the prediction by the Japanese Navy General Staff that by 1942 the United States would have achieved an unassailable dominance in the Pacific. The Japanese Navy desperately needed the oil in the Dutch East Indies, while the Army wanted to cut off Chinese supply lines that ran through parts of South-East Asia. A neutrality pact was duly signed with the Soviet Union in April 1941, and a few months later, with France now under Nazi control, Japanese troops occupied French Indochina.

Talks were held with the United States, in hopes of avoiding further escalation. But the Americans wanted the Japanese out of China, and this was simply not within Konoe's gift: neither the Army nor public opinion would permit it. Konoe resigned in despair in the autumn of 1941 and was replaced as prime minister by General Tōjō Hideki. Soon afterwards, the decision was made that further negotiations with the United States would be fruitless. Conflict was now inevitable. The only question was how Japan, as the weaker power, should approach it.

The answer to that question arrived over the Hawaiian island of Oahu early in the morning on Sunday 7 December 1941, in the form of 350 Japanese fighters and bombers. Intelligence officers working for the Japanese Navy had been scouting potential targets for some time, driving and even flying around the island to track the habitual movements of US Navy vessels in and out of Pearl Harbor along with the positioning of aircraft and hangars at sites including Wheeler Army Airfield.

Japan's surprise attack on Pearl Harbor was at once a great success and a highly consequential failure. It was extraordinary that six Japanese carriers had made it to within 200 miles of Oahu's northern coast without being detected and that two large waves of aircraft had been launched in quick succession, entirely overwhelming American defences. Around 2,400 Americans were killed, five American battleships were lost and around 200 aircraft were destroyed. But much of the US Navy's crucial infrastructure at Pearl Harbor survived, as did the three aircraft carriers operating in the region, all of which were elsewhere at the time. That meant that when the hoped-for peace overtures from the United States failed to materialise, and in their place a deep and dramatic anti-Japanese sentiment took hold, the US Navy was able to start exacting punishment far more quickly and effectively than Japanese strategists anticipated.

The Allied response to Pearl Harbor and to Japan's

declaration of war on the United States and the British Empire took a few months to get going. In that time, Japanese forces enjoyed rapid successes, capturing a string of colonial territories in South-East Asia by mid-1942: Hong Kong, Manila, Malaya, Singapore, Rangoon, Java and Guadalcanal. Thereafter, Japan's war went steadily downhill. The United States outstripped the Japanese in the quantity and quality of industrial production for the war effort, while its submarines devastated Japan's maritime supply lines.

A key moment was reached in July 1944, when the fall of Saipan to the Allies prompted Tōjō Hideki's resignation and brought the Japanese home islands within range for large-scale air raids. The war was already keenly felt in Japan, in everything from food rationing and the closure of entertainment venues to requirements to dress simply, organise into neighbourhood associations (whose participants effectively spied on one another) and surrender pots, pans and other items to be melted down for the production of armour and bullets. People were told to expect an Allied invasion, in preparation for which they were drilled in the use of bamboo spears. Still, the air raids brought the war home to ordinary Japanese as never before. The most destructive sortie in history hit Tokyo on 9 March 1945, destroying a quarter of the city and killing around 100,000 people. Most of Japan's other major cities were bombed, too, and for the authorities morale among the general public was a mounting concern. The vast majority of Japanese kept their counsel but the Special Higher Police uncovered evidence of sedition – including threatening letters written to the emperor – and of growing sympathy for communist ideals.

While seeking to keep foreign ideologies at bay, Japan's leaders reached back into their own history for inspiration as the war reached its climax. From Classical Chinese poetry, they drew the idea that 'a true man would rather be the shattered jewel, ashamed to be the intact tile'. Japan was to be a country, now, of 'one hundred million shattered jewels', each person proving their value in the moment of sacrifice. From the era of the failed Mongol invasions came romantic imagery for a desperate, last-ditch tactic. A 'Divine Wind Special Attack Force' was created in the autumn of 1944, and a total of around 3,300 planes were sent on 'kamikaze' missions over the months that followed: packed with explosives and flown directly at Allied shipping. Young men, many of whom had been coerced into volunteering, were given cheerful runway send-offs by groups of girls waving cherry blossom branches – their brief period of bloom made them natural symbols of short but beautiful lives. Pilot letters and diaries published after the war revealed a sense of profound resignation among some of these young men: history had brought them to the point where their only option was to play their part in Japan's demise. The most they could hope for, as one put it, was to help burn the field, making it fertile once again for a future generation.

The kamikaze tactic enjoyed a brief period of success when it was first used. But the Allies adapted quickly, and although hundreds of American vessels were either sunk or damaged by kamikaze attacks there was never much prospect of them changing the course of the war. Former Prime Minister Konoe Fumimarō hoped to achieve that instead by suggesting to the emperor, in February 1945, that defeat was now inevitable and it would be better to end the conflict quickly rather than let the threat of communist revolution in Japan continue to grow. Konoe's gambit failed – the emperor was unpersuaded, and the military police, concerned about defeatism, placed Konoe under surveillance. The war went on, reaching a bloody climax in April 1945 at the Battle of Okinawa. More than 12,000 American servicemen and 110,000 Japanese troops died in ferocious fighting across the island. Suicide charges by Japanese soldiers and the forced suicide of civilians – tens of thousands of whom perished in the space of just a few weeks – helped to reinforce a fear among American military planners that its adversary was willing to sacrifice both its military men and the wider population in defending Japan's home islands. It was clear that a full-scale invasion would come at an unacceptable cost in American lives.

The hope in Japan, at this late hour, was that the Soviet Union might mediate with the other Allies on Japan's behalf. But by the time of the Potsdam Conference in July 1945, the Soviet Union had already agreed to enter the war against Japan. While at Potsdam, US President Truman received word both of Japan's hope of Russian mediation and of the successful test of the world's first atomic bomb. On 26 July, the Potsdam Declaration called for Japan's unconditional surrender, threatening it otherwise with 'prompt and utter destruction'. The intentions of a postwar occupation were laid out, including the disarming of the military, the trial of suspected war criminals and the institution of freedoms of speech, religion and thought in Japan.

The imperial palace in Tokyo had so far been spared any

bombing by the Allies, on the basis that the death of the emperor would only strengthen the will of ordinary Japanese to fight. But the Potsdam Declaration failed to make any mention of what would happen to the emperor if Japan surrendered, making it easier for those in the Japanese armed forces who were opposed to ending the war to continue to have their way. Instead, it took a catastrophic few days in early August finally to bring the conflict to a close. On 6 August, news reached Tokyo of a devastating new mystery weapon used against Hiroshima: a single bomb, which had wiped out parts of the city completely and turned much of what remained into a flaming hell. On 8 August, the Soviet Union responded to Japan's hopes of mediation with a declaration of war. Then on 9 August, as Soviet troops began to pour into Japanese-held Manchuria, a second bomb was dropped on Nagasaki – raising the prospect that the Allies might have many more in their possession.

Even at this point, some of Japan's military leaders refused to countenance giving in. In the end, the emperor was asked to make a decision, and he chose surrender. On 15 August, the people of Japan heard his voice for the first time over the radio, as he read out an Imperial Rescript accepting the terms of the Potsdam Declaration. The language used was that of the ancient imperial court, and some listeners did not understand what was being said. Those who did heard the emperor tell his subjects that they had been fighting a war for the preservation of Japan, but that the war had begun to go against them and the enemy was now using a 'new and most cruel bomb'. In order to save Japan and avoid the 'total extinction of human civilisation', the Japanese must lay down their arms. This would not, however, said the emperor, be the end:

> Let the entire nation continue as one family from generation to generation, ever firm in its faith in the imperishability of its sacred land, and mindful of its heavy burden of responsibility, and of the long road before it.

# CHAPTER 9

# The Bright Life

Back in the late 1850s, when international pressure was mounting on Japan to open up treaty ports for trade, the Tokugawa shogunate had concluded that although it lacked the strength to keep the foreigners out, by anticipating their desires it might exert some modest control over events. The result was the thriving port of Yokohama, whose shops, restaurants and brothels helped to quarantine Japan's unwanted guests. The country's leaders took a similar approach in the summer of 1945, starting the process of complying with the terms of the Potsdam Declaration before the occupation even began, in hopes of softening its impact and even steering its course to Japan's advantage. An imperial order was issued, disbanding the armed forces. The Ministry of Munitions was shut down. Incriminating government documents were burned, adding to a haze over Tokyo created by vehicles converted to run on charcoal, wood and household rubbish. And old plans for land and labour reform were resurrected.

While all this was going on, ordinary Japanese were beginning to come to terms with the devastation wrought by the war. To add to more than 2 million deaths in the Japanese military, half a million civilians had perished and 9 million more were now homeless. Cholera, typhoid, polio and dysentery had taken hold, alongside widespread hunger. In Hiroshima, as many as 140,000 people were either dead or dying from the effects of the world's first atomic bombing. Buildings, trees, even the streets themselves had been ignited by the blast. Bodies had melted into the ground; others had transformed into human silhouettes eerily imprinted on to walls. As radiation sickness began to take hold, people went in search of combinations of herbs that might treat the fevers and the hair loss. At Nagasaki, once Japan's gateway to the world, around 70,000 people suffered the same awful fate.

Across Japan, desperate survivors of the war sought out the black markets that were beginning to proliferate. Swelled by food, fuel and clothing looted from government stockpiles intended to support a years-long battle to defend the home islands, many of these were run by *yakuza* gangsters. The word came from a losing hand in a Japanese card game: *ya* (8), *ku* (9), *za* (3). Another option for starving city-dwellers was to head out to the countryside to barter with farmers for the basics. Photographs taken during the weeks and months after surrender show packed-out trains with people hanging on to the roof and off the sides. Hundreds of thousands of people made journeys like these every day from Tokyo alone: a grim, potentially combustible situation that was made worse as millions of demobilised soldiers and colonial civil servants began to make their way home.

On 2 September 1945, a formal Instrument of Surrender was signed aboard the USS *Missouri* in Tokyo Bay. One of the flags on the battleship had been flying over the White House on the day that Pearl Harbor was attacked. Another had been flown by Commodore Matthew C. Perry back in 1853. The

Allied Occupation of Japan, dominated by the United States and in particular by General Douglas MacArthur as Supreme Commander of the Allied Powers (SCAP), had at its heart a strong sense of history. Japan, it was thought, had undergone an impressive but incomplete process of modernisation in the late nineteenth century. A feudal mindset had survived, causing democracy to fall prey to militarism and emperor mysticism. The purpose of the Occupation was to correct these mistakes, remaking Japan more or less in America's image.

Plenty of people in Japan were willing to go along with this interpretation of the past, in whole or in part. Feminists like Ichikawa Fusae wanted to see women, at last, get the vote. Communists urged people to embrace the Occupation as the next stage in Japan's history. The political scientist Maruyama Masao made the influential case that individual will and conscience had been effaced under Japan's old political arrangements. The result was that too few people had been willing to voice their opposition to bad and dangerous ideas. It was now time to nurture a fresh balance, in the population, of self-sufficiency and public commitment.

A first official draft of recent history was created by the International Military Tribunal for the Far East, which convened in Tokyo in April 1946 and which would come to be known as the Tokyo Trials. Eleven judges drawn from the Allied nations sat in a courtroom hearing testimony about the activities of senior Japanese leaders as far back as 1928: the date chosen as the starting point for the political and military plots that had given rise to the war and its associated crimes. Ishiwara Kanji, called as a witness, suggested that Commodore Perry's fateful exercise in gunboat diplomacy would be a better place to start.

Tōjō Hideki, on trial for his life, suggested the Opium Wars of the mid-nineteenth century, given the role of British imperialism in shaping the region.

Decisions had to be made, too, about which aspects of the war the tribunal would and would not explore. It was decided that Emperor Hirohito would not be placed on trial: he was essential in securing Japanese co-operation with the aims of the Occupation. Nor would the activities be considered of the Imperial Japanese Army's infamous Unit 731, a biological warfare unit based in Manchuria whose grisly research included human vivisection. Its senior personnel were offered immunity in exchange for what was regarded by the United States as valuable scientific data. Allied conduct during the war was also placed beyond the purview of the tribunal, including the dropping of atomic bombs on Hiroshima and Nagasaki.

The tribunal's workings and later reputation suffered both from contentious decisions like these and the destruction of key evidence, not least concerning the slaughter and rape visited upon the city of Nanjing by Japanese troops in the winter of 1937–8. Few Chinese could afford to travel to Japan to give first-hand testimony, and affidavits proved a poor substitute. Added to this were the vicissitudes of the courtroom, which saw the chief prosecutor Joseph Keenan fail to deal convincingly with Tōjō Hideki. Keenan took over at the last minute from a better-prepared junior, and the results were embarrassing. Tōjō was the one living under threat of the noose. But, as a woman working in the British embassy put it, 'Tōjō had a good morning hanging Keenan.' He managed to cast much of Keenan's evidence into doubt and to make the claim – later repeated down the decades by ultra-nationalists in Japan – that his country had acted in self-defence against encircling enemies.

When the tribunal delivered its verdict, in November 1948, twenty-five defendants were each found guilty on at least one count. Seven, including Tōjō, were sentenced to death. Japanese newspapers covered the proceedings in detail, helping to generate an atmosphere of justice being seen to be done. But the Indian judge, Radhabinod Pal, issued a damaging dissenting opinion in which he described the tribunal as 'formalised vengeance'. The Chinese judge, Mei Ju-ao, criticised what he saw as a scapegoat strategy: limiting war responsibility to a small 'group of evil culprits', in hopes of recruiting everyone else to help build a new Japan. A similar strategy played out on the radio, where an Occupation-sponsored series called *Now It Can Be Told*, broadcast in 1945–6, offered a distinctly one-sided 'real story' of the war to Japanese listeners. It received so many complaints that it had to be cancelled.

Rather than encourage a broad reckoning with the past, of the sort that Japan's victims across Asia would have liked to see, the Occupation authorities preferred to look to the future. They sought to work with the Japanese government and civil service to implement their reforms as swiftly and smoothly as possible. The process of disbanding the armed forces was quickly completed, and Japan was relieved of its former colonial possessions, from Korea and Manchuria to Taiwan and out into the Pacific. *Zaibatsu* assets were broken up, in the name of economic democratisation: the 'Big Four' alone – Mitsui, Mitsubishi, Sumitomo and Yasuda – had at one point controlled a third of Japanese heavy industry and half of the country's finance and insurance. Five million tenant farmers were awarded ownership of their land. And tens of thousands of people deemed to have been complicit in 'Japanese aggression or militant nationalism' were purged from public life, including journalists, businessmen, teachers, publishers and police. Civil servants were largely spared, since their expertise was deemed essential. All that was required of senior figures was that they sit an examination to test their fitness for office. Dubbed the 'Paradise Exam', candidates were given an unlimited amount of time, alongside free tea and cigarettes to spur them on.

Valiant yet doomed attempts were made by the Japanese government to limit democratic reform to some tinkering with the 1889 Meiji Constitution. Instead, in 1946 Japan became the first country in history to have its constitution drafted by a foreign power. The new document was introduced to the Japanese public via a cheery illustrated pamphlet titled 'New Constitution, Bright Life'. The emperor, they learned, was to be stripped of his authority and turned into a 'symbol' of the nation. Power would be handed to the people: men and women would elect representatives to a new bicameral Diet, and the largest party in the lower house would select the prime minister. Executive authority would rest with a cabinet, responsible to the Diet. Local governments would gain enhanced powers, and the judiciary would be made fully independent. The Constitution also guaranteed a range of inalienable rights, including education, public health and collective bargaining for workers. Religion and state were to remain separate: there was to be no repeat of what the Americans regarded as the pernicious connections forged between Shintō, the emperor and ultra-nationalism.

The making of war, alongside the maintaining of the means to do so, was renounced forever.

Opinion polls revealed broad public support for these new measures, and MacArthur personally was treated with a certain awe as the 'Blue-Eyed Shogun' – even by his own Occupation staff, some of whom joked that if you got up early in the morning you would see MacArthur out on the moat of the imperial palace, walking on the water. But there were those in Japan who regarded the Americans as going beyond the inescapable basics of an occupation and waging a culture war on their defeated enemy. A case in point was the emperor's 'Declaration of Humanity' on New Year's Day in 1946. Japanese people were urged to put behind them the 'false conception that the Emperor is divine', along with all its attendant 'legends and myths'. The idea for this declaration was said to have come from among the emperor's own advisors, as part of their strategy of ensuring that the Allies did not do away with the institution entirely. Some Japanese conservatives regarded it as a humiliation nonetheless, along with the abolition of the old household system, the awarding of new rights to women and a series of education reforms that emphasised peaceful internationalism at the expense of pride in Japan.

Clumsy Occupation attempts to censor the arts in Japan had the effect of reinforcing such arguments. Everyone from haiku poets to *kabuki* actors and film-makers faced having their work altered or banned on the basis that it was 'too feudal' or else constituted 'criticism of the United States'. Letters and packages were opened and checked. Telephone calls were subject to eavesdropping. And half-hearted attempts were made to balance out bowing as a form of greeting – again, 'too feudal' – with more hand-shaking and kissing. More seriously, efforts were made to keep from the Japanese public the truth of what had happened at Hiroshima and Nagasaki. When a Catholic doctor named Nagai Takashi published his memoir of the bombing of Nagasaki – *Nagasaki no Kane* (*The Bells of Nagasaki*, 1949) – his publishers were forced to include in the book, for the sake of 'balance', an American-authored appendix detailing the Japanese Army's 'Sack of Manila', in which 100,000 civilians were killed.

Japan's leftists and liberals were, by contrast, delighted with the achievements of the first two years of the Occupation. Their joy, however, was short-lived. MacArthur, along with policy-makers back in the United States, was becoming increasingly concerned about the potential for hunger and homelessness in Japan to be exploited by communist leaders like Tokuda Kyūichi. In May 1946, Tokuda had addressed a rally of 200,000 people near the imperial palace. 'We are starving!' he shouted to his supporters, before turning around to point at the palace – 'Is he?' The next year, MacArthur intervened to ban a national strike planned for 1 February, in which up to 2.6 million people were set to take part.

In the face of this radicalism, along with worsening US–Soviet relationships and the threat – realised in the autumn of 1949 – of communist revolution in China, the United States decided to shift its stance on Japan. The plan, henceforth, would be to prioritise the health of Japan's economy, turning the country into a reliable trading partner and ally against communism. As part of what came to be called the 'reverse course', left-wing elements in Japanese society were purged, attitudes hardened towards trades unions and ongoing efforts to break up economic monopolies were set aside. When the Korean War broke out in 1950, the United States helped to equip a new National Police Reserve (NPR) in Japan. Its official remit was to keep the peace while American troops stationed in Japan for that purpose went off to fight in Korea. But the US envisaged it becoming the nucleus of a future Japanese army. Within a few short years the NPR had morphed into the Self-Defence Forces, setting in train decades of anguished discussion about the circumstances in which they might be deployed.

In September 1951, Japan and forty-eight nations, including former victims and enemies, signed the San Francisco Peace Treaty. The loss of Japan's colonies was confirmed, the Ryukyu Islands – old Okinawa prefecture – were placed in American trusteeship and limited reparations were agreed. Absent from the peace conference were the two Koreas, still at war, and two Chinas: the new People's Republic and the old Republic, the latter hunkering down on the island of Taiwan.

The Soviet Union sent representatives to the peace conference but declined to sign the treaty, having failed to achieve key objectives, including the removal of all foreign troops from Japanese soil. The United States could not accept this condition: it would have undermined a bilateral security treaty signed with Japan shortly after the peace treaty was concluded. This second treaty provided for the maintenance of American military bases on Japanese soil and even for intervention by American forces to quell domestic unrest in Japan. Japan benefited from having its security underwritten by the United States, but the price paid in the compromise of its independence was high, not least in foreign policy where it was forbidden from forging diplomatic relations with Mao's China.

After the Occupation came to an end, on 28 April 1952, it fell to a wily and far-sighted political operator named Yoshida Shigeru to navigate these difficult waters. A former Foreign Ministry bureaucrat who had joined Konoe Fumimarō in begging the emperor to end the war early – spending some time in jail for his trouble – Yoshida entered the postwar era with impeccable connections and comparative freedom from the taint of Japanese war-mongering. He also offered a more optimistic reading of recent history than the Americans. The Meiji and Taishō eras, together spanning 1868 to 1926, should be understood in terms not of half-baked modernisation and prelude to disaster but remarkable achievement. What followed was an aberration, from which the Japanese could best recover not by adopting American life wholesale but by returning to that earlier sense of pride and purpose.

When Japan went to the polls for the first time since the war in April 1946, women now voting alongside men for the first time, a newly formed conservative party called Jiyūtō (Liberal Party), descended from the pre-war Seiyūkai, emerged victorious. Yoshida was not a member, but when the wartime record of Jiyūtō's leader saw him banned from taking up the post of prime minister, Yoshida was invited to take the post instead. He ended up serving as prime minister almost uninterrupted from May 1946 through to December 1954.

Dubbed the 'pocket Churchill' for his Anglophilia, love of cigars, diminutive stature and deep suspicion of the Left, Yoshida helped to set Japan's political and economic course for decades to come. He made the most of the American alliance while pushing back against the more excessive American demands for Japan to rearm. And he oversaw the formation – or rather, re-formation – of an 'iron triangle' consisting of conservative politicians, civil servants and banks and big business. Together, they co-ordinated Japan's economic recovery, coming up with policies and tax breaks that would help funnel scarce capital into the industries of the future: iron, steel, chemicals, electronics and automobiles. A new Ministry for International Trade and Industry (MITI) became emblematic of a desire in Japan to see economic nationalism take the place of the previous, bloodier sort. Some of MITI's bureaucrats adopted for their protectionist motto the old Tokugawa slogan: 'Expel the barbarian!'

The Korean War, too, played its part in Japan's recovery. It ended badly for MacArthur, who was chosen to serve as Commander-in-Chief of the United Nations forces but was relieved of both that position and his job in Japan after he tried to turn the war into a wider attack on China. But the Japanese economy received a much-needed shot in the arm thanks to US military procurement orders worth between 2 and 4 billion dollars. Yoshida described it as a 'gift from the gods'.

A handful of pre war Japanese companies soon began to establish themselves as household names, domestically and later internationally, including Nissan, Toshiba, Hitachi and Panasonic. A notable newcomer was the Tokyo Telecommunications Engineering Company. It started life as a single Datsun truck trundling around Tokyo on black market fuel delivering electrical parts before moving on to inventing and marketing – largely without success – a thirty-five-kilogram tape recorder. Persistent lobbying of MITI eventually resulted in permission to purchase a manufacturing licence for American transistor technology. Thanks to smaller products and a more compact name to match, 'Sony' went on to become a symbol of Japan's remarkable comeback. The name was very much a product of this period: gleaned from a combination of *sonus*, the Latin for 'sound', and the phrase 'sonny boy', beloved of American GIs in Japan.

The basic bargain at the heart of the 'Yoshida Doctrine', peace and prosperity in return for the partial subordination of Japanese to American interests, helped Japan's economy to grow by an average of more than 10 per cent every year from 1953 through to the early 1970s. By the end of that period, the overwhelming majority of Japanese considered themselves to be 'middle class': sufficiently affluent to be able to afford a decent home, a car, the latest electronic goods and a holiday now and again. *The Economist* magazine dubbed it an 'economic miracle'.

Against this backdrop of rapidly increasing national wealth, Tokyo's hosting of the Summer Olympics in 1964 turned into something of a public relations coup for the new Japan. Spectators came in from all over the world to marvel at a city reborn, superfast *shinkansen* trains – designed by former army and navy personnel and launched to coincide with the Games – immaculately organised events, and most of all what the British sports journalist Chris Brasher called the 'hard work, humility and charm' of the Japanese. Japan's national flag and anthem came to be associated now with casualty-free sporting competition and even the Self-Defence Forces managed to win for themselves a little warmth from a still-wavering Japanese public. They provided security for the Olympics, contributed athletes to some of the events – including the winner of a gold medal in weightlifting – and dazzled the crowds with an aerobatics display, performed by the SDF display team 'Blue Impulse'.

And yet, for all that Japan's mainstream media preferred to celebrate the 'bright life' rather than dwell too much on the past, there were misgivings among a great many Japanese about their country's postwar direction of travel. In 1955, Japan's conservative parties had come together to form the Liberal Democratic Party (LDP): Jiyū-Minshutō, or Jimintō for short. So dominant did the new party become that the most consequential debates within Japanese politics ended up happening not between competing parties but within the ranks of the LDP. The pre-war trend of having bureaucrats cross over into politics meanwhile continued. During his time as prime minister, Yoshida managed to recruit two future prime ministers into politics from the civil service: Ikeda Hayato (prime minister 1960–64) and Satō Eisaku (1964–72). Whether or not one liked such men and their policies, it was clear that Japan's reinvention as a lively and broad-based democracy had stalled.

Or had it? There was more to democracy than goings-on behind closed doors in Tokyo's government quarter. Across the 1950s, 60s and 70s, a range of controversies emerged around which citizens made sure that their voices were heard. One of the earliest was the continued presence of American military bases on Japanese soil. Critics claimed that a culture of alcohol, sexualised music, petty crime and prostitution grew up around the bases and that Japan risked being turned into a nuclear target by the Soviet Union. When attempts were made to expand Tachikawa air base near Tokyo in 1955, the people of a nearby village, Sunagawa, rose up to oppose the plans. They soon found students, artists, left-wing politicians, trades unions and even a number of Buddhist priests from across Japan arriving to join them in their protests. In 1959, a judge in a Tokyo district court handed down the sensational ruling that the presence of US military bases on Japanese soil was unlawful under the very constitution that the Americans themselves had written for Japan. The Supreme Court swiftly intervened to quash the ruling, but plans to expand Tachikawa air base ended up being shelved.

Nuclear weapons themselves became a magnet for Japanese activism. No country on earth could match Japan for moral authority on this question, which was tied to people's feelings about the United States both because of the bombings at Hiroshima and Nagasaki and because of America's continued testing of weapons in Japan's backyard. In the spring of 1954, the crew of a Japanese fishing boat called the *Lucky Dragon 5* were irradiated during an American weapons test at Bikini Atoll in the mid-Pacific. One fisherman died, others suffered serious injuries and panic spread in Japan about contaminated catches. Later that year, *Gojira* was released in Japanese cinemas, starring a towering monster – its name a portmanteau of the Japanese words for 'gorilla' and 'whale' – who is awakened from its sleep by American nuclear testing in the Pacific. The film's director, Honda Ishirō, had seen for himself the devastation at Hiroshima and imagined Gojira, or Godzilla, as nuclear disaster 'made flesh'.

Godzilla was intended as an allegory for nuclear power in general, rather than American (mis)use of the technology in particular. Japan's anti-nuclear movement, too, sought to be internationalist and peaceful in tone right from its inception in 1955, when a newly opened Hiroshima Memorial Peace Museum hosted the first World Conference Against Atomic and Hydrogen Bombs. Still, public anger at the United States' overbearing treatment of Japan and at their own supine politicians contributed to a tense atmosphere in the run-up to revision of the US–Japan Security Treaty in 1960.

Japan's prime minister at the time, Kishi Nobusuke, was already unpopular. As the Japanese Empire's highest-ranking bureaucrat in Manchukuo in the pre-war years, he had become involved in money-laundering, slave labour, drug trafficking and consorting with *yakuza*. After the war, he spent three years in Sugamo Prison before being released without trial. As prime minister, he had already tried to return to Japan's police forces their old powers to enter private property whenever they pleased and without needing a warrant. This high-handedness continued in May 1960 when the renewal of the security treaty – dubbed 'Anpo' in Japanese – was due to pass through the Diet. As people surrounded the building and Socialist Party members tried to trap the Speaker of the House in his chambers, Kishi used the police to drag away his political enemies and allow the measure to pass unopposed.

Chaos ensued, as hundreds of thousands of protestors thronged the streets and millions of people took part in strike action. A planned visit by US President Dwight D. Eisenhower had to be cancelled, and when a Tokyo University student, Kanba Michiko, was killed in a confrontation with riot police even more protestors joined the anti-Anpo movement. Kishi's resignation eventually took some of the heat out of the protests, but for a short time it looked as though Japan's Self-Defence Forces might be called on to intervene – setting a very dangerous precedent for Japan's fledgling democracy. The stabbing to death on live television later that year of a prominent Socialist Party politician, Asanuma Inejirō, only added to a sense that Japan might, at any time, return to the turbulence and political violence of the past.

In the end, the Anpo protests died down and the passing of the renewed treaty was allowed to stand. The LDP continued to shore up its base with rice price regulation to protect farmers and a light-touch taxation regime for small businesses. The population at large was meanwhile promised in 1960 that incomes would double within a decade. This extraordinarily ambitious target was hit early, in 1967, and the next year Japan overtook West Germany to become the world's second-largest economy after the United States.

Critics charged that Japan was slipping into affluent complacency. But even prosperity generated opportunities for activism. Women's groups hauled companies over the coals for producing inferior or dangerous products, including tainted cooking oil. A National Conference on Children's Culture forced the Recording Industry Association of Japan to adopt an ethics code, pledging that an increasingly lucrative pop industry would promote wholesome living and avoid the glorification of crime, indecency or anything that threatened 'child psychology'. And in 1970, environmentalists successfully used the tragedy of Minamata disease, caused by factory effluent, to win more stringent environmental regulations for Japan than almost anywhere in the world. Local politics, too, proved to be a promising means of circumventing disappointment at the national level. The Socialist Party politician Minobe Ryōkichi served as governor of Tokyo from 1967 all the way through to 1979, using his record-breaking tenure to clean up Tokyo's streets, improve its public services and provide free health insurance to elderly residents who could not afford it.

The late 1960s and early 1970s meanwhile witnessed one last gasp for radical politics in Japan. University students were among those to critique the idea that economic growth was sufficient as a national purpose. The result, they said, was a school education that felt like 'living in handcuffs', followed by university classes that were boring, expensive and shaped by the needs of the country's employers rather than having any higher aim in view. These grievances came together with opposition to the war in Vietnam to bring thousands of students out in protest in 1968 and 1969, shutting down parts of Tokyo and requiring the use of riot police, water cannon and tear gas to bring the situation under control.

In 1970, samurai swords made a brief return to public consciousness. They were used in March of that year, along with dummy pipe bombs, to help the Japanese communist group the Red Army Faction hijack a commercial flight somewhere above Mount Fuji. The group hoped to get to Cuba, but after a few days of stopovers and tense runway negotiations had to make do with North Korea, where the authorities turned them into intelligence assets. Some were still living there fifty years later. In November 1970, the novelist, playwright and sometime member of the Self-Defence Forces Mishima Yukio staged the greatest drama of his career. For a while, the SDF had regarded a legendary writer joining their ranks as a great propaganda coup. But on 25 November Mishima tried to stage an actual coup, leading four members of his private militia into a pre-arranged meeting with the commandant of an SDF barracks in Tokyo. Mishima gave a speech from the commandant's balcony to bewildered recruits below, castigating postwar Japan for its 'spiritual emptiness' and calling on them to hurl their bodies against the constitution. Failing to get the hoped-for response, Mishima returned to the commandant's office and performed *seppuku*. A member of his militia acted as his 'second' and removed his head.

Mishima Yukio's violent death, followed by televised footage in early 1972 of remnants of the Red Army Faction fighting a gun battle with police at their mountain hideout, helped to persuade the Japanese general public of the virtues of pragmatism over big-picture radicalism in politics. Social criticism did not go away. Ōya Sōichi denounced the 'nation of 100 million idiots' that television seemed to be creating – he likened watching TV to spotting two dogs mating on a street corner: compulsive viewing, but you felt stupid afterwards. Hidaka Rokurō meanwhile worried that Japan was becoming a 'controlled society' as wealth, combined with the homogenising effects of education and the mainstream media, yielded a population all living the same, standardised lives marked by simple pleasures and political quietism. Increasingly, however, grand visions of the future – from utopian fantasies to apocalyptic disasters intended as cautionary tales – were confined mostly to film, television dramas, anime and manga. Popular culture was thriving in Japan, and beginning to emerge as a major postwar export.

Leading the charge was Tezuka Osamu, Japan's 'godfather

of manga'. People had been creating manga – 'whimsical pictures' – at least as far back as the twelfth century, when the Tendai Buddhist monk Toba Sōjō produced some or all of a picture scroll called *Chōjū Giga* (*Animal Caricatures*). A mixture of fun and satire, the scroll shows frogs, rabbits and other animals engaged in human pursuits: feasting, playing games and attending a funeral at which a monkey dressed in Buddhist robes officiates. Another of Toba's works showed men gorging on sweet potatoes, fuelling up for a 'Fart Battle'. In the Edo and Meiji eras, artists like Kawanabe Kyōsai could be found carrying on this tradition of entertainment combined with light-hearted political commentary. New magazines emerged, including *Japan Punch* and *Tokyo Puck*, which fused Japanese tradition with the western political cartoon. Kitazawa Rakuten (1876–1955) became the first to claim for himself the mantle of 'manga artist', creating a comic strip about two simple country folk bowled over by big-city life.

To these influences Tezuka added his love of Disney and his hatred for what Japan's leaders had put the country through during the war. He had been a medical student in Osaka during its final months, and after air raids hit the city had seen dead bodies floating down the Yodogawa River. Deciding on manga rather than medicine for his career, Tezuka set out to use his art both to entertain – publishers sought Japanese answers to American comics like *Batman* and *Superman* – and to ensure that children understood how corrupt the adult world could be. His most famous hero was Astro Boy: a crime-fighting child-robot with large Betty Boop-like eyes and shiny black hair. Clothed in black shorts and red boots, he had an atomic reactor in his chest, powering his computer brain, searchlight eyes and jets built into his arms and feet.

Suitably sanitised for American children in the 1960s – Tezuka's studio was forced by the broadcaster NBC to tone down some of the violence – Astro Boy became part of a gradual revision of Japan in western minds. The samurai films of Kurosawa Akira played their part, too. Never quite as big a name at home in Japan as he was in the West, Kurosawa presented samurai culture to western audiences as dignified and chivalrous, spiced with an earthy sense of humour and sometimes reaching Shakespearean heights of drama – literally so in 1957's *Throne of Blood*, which transposed *Macbeth* from medieval Scotland to Japan in the era of the Warring States. The director Yasujirō Ozu made a name for himself in the West, too, with *Tokyo Story* (1953): an elegy to quiet, quotidian Japanese domesticity.

Thanks to Tezuka and Kurosawa, alongside the Godzilla franchise, westerners began to imagine the people of Japan less as the automaton butchers and slavers of the Second World War and more as lovers of cutesy cartoon characters, giant rubber monsters wrestling one another and disciplined, justice-seeking swordsmen. The Japanese government added a layer of its own, circumventing recent history by portraying Japan as a place of timeless high culture. The great classical age of Murasaki Shikibu and Sei Shōnagon was celebrated for its literature, fashion, poetry and painting. Art forms that emphasised care, calm, accuracy and effort were offered up for export, from *ikebana* (flower-arranging) to calligraphy.

Western writers played their own part in this resurgence of interest in Japan. James Clavell's novel *Shogun*

(1975) turned the story of William Adams, the first English-man in Japan, into a swashbuckling fantasy that sold 7 million copies in five years. *Japan as Number One: Lessons for America* (1979), by the Harvard sociologist Ezra Vogel, meanwhile helped to entrench the idea that a culture of hard work, labour-management co-operation and enlightened public policies had rendered postwar Japan unbeatable on the business battlefield.

Welcome though prosperity and changing western perceptions of Japan undoubtedly were, the Japanese continued to lament the sometimes poor quality of their political leadership. In 1971, US President Richard Nixon announced on television that he would be visiting the People's Republic of China the following year. The fact that no one in the US administration felt the need to discuss this momentous shift in American foreign policy with their Japanese allies ahead of time served to highlight the subordinate relationship that Japan's politicians continued to tolerate for their country. Nixon also announced a New Economic Program, whose impact on Japanese exports to America was disastrous. Two years later, in 1973, Japan's heavy reliance on Middle Eastern oil was exposed when prices briefly quadrupled, causing people to rush out to raid supermarket shelves in fear of price rises and scarcity.

And then there was all the corruption. The downside to having an 'iron triangle' of LDP politicians, civil servants and big business run the country was that the line between pragmatic co-operation and pork-barrel politics could become awfully thin. No one was more closely associated with this world than Tanaka Kakuei, postwar Japan's answer to Fujiwara no Michinaga. Both men knew how to make friends, pull strings and tuck away tidy profits for themselves. Where Michinaga had had the imperial court dancing to his tune, Tanaka Kakuei did the same with the vast machinery of the LDP.

Tanaka entered top-tier politics in 1957, handing Prime Minister Kishi Nobusuke a backpack stuffed with 3 million yen in cash, in exchange for which he was appointed to his first cabinet post as minister of posts and telecommunications. He proved to be a master of the *kōenkai* system, which involved candidates building around themselves strong local bases of business support and rewarding them with contracts and tax breaks once in office. Tanaka's particular approach was to play up his outsider status. In an era when most of Japan's political elites came from prominent families and had passed through the same handful of top universities, Tanaka hailed from rural Niigata prefecture, on Honshū's chilly north-western coast, and had left school at the age of fourteen. He managed to combine his unusual back story with a critique of Japan's uneven economic development since the 1950s. Money and people, he claimed, had been funnelled into Pacific Belt cities like Tokyo, Nagoya, Osaka and Fukuoka. The result was overcrowding and high levels of pollution in these favoured places while other parts of Japan were left behind.

In 1972, Tanaka produced his blueprint for changing all this. *A Plan for Remodelling the Japanese Archipelago* (*Nihon Rettō Kaizō Ron*) was one of the first attempts to set out a vision for Japan now that the era of high economic growth was coming to an end. Tanaka called for new cities to be created and for the introduction to the countryside of high-tech farming and new forms of entertainment as a way of stemming the tide of young people leaving for the big cities. With the fruits of economic growth distributed more evenly, a wave of 'spiritual affluence' would sweep Japan, he said, helping it to stand up for itself abroad.

Tanaka's election as LDP leader in 1972 made it seem as though Japan really might be heading in a new direction, a sense heightened by Tanaka's history-making meeting with Mao Zedong and Zhou Enlai in Beijing in September of that year. Mao and Tanaka bonded over their rustic roots and love of East Asian culture, a normalisation agreement was signed, and Sino-Japanese trade began rapidly to increase – from $1 billion in 1972 to $4 billion in 1975. Tanaka's approval ratings at home briefly topped 60 per cent, and the *New York Times* compared him with Franklin D. Roosevelt. Then came the oil shock of 1973 and rumours that Tanaka had bought up property in Niigata prefecture whose value he knew was about to increase because of infrastructure investment there. Some of the transactions were hidden from scrutiny by using other people's names on key documents – including, in one case, that of Tanaka's favourite geisha. Set alongside evidence of excessive clientelism in the 1974 elections, the pressure became too much for Tanaka, and he resigned in November of that year.

This was by no means the end for Tanaka. Japan's constitution placed executive authority in the hands of the cabinet rather than the prime minister, and by using his *kōenkai* network to control enough cabinet members Tanaka found that, like a cloistered emperor from centuries before, he could effectively run the country from his lavishly appointed private estate. Little changed even when evidence emerged in 1976 that while still prime minister Tanaka had taken an enormous bribe from the American aerospace company

Lockheed to persuade All Nippon Airways to choose one of its planes for its fleet over a rival model produced by McDonnell Douglas. Tanaka became the first person to be charged with criminal abuse of the prime minister's office, but by the time a court found him guilty in 1983 he could claim to have as many as one in four LDP Diet members in his pocket. Such was his sway over Prime Minister Nakasone Yasuhiro in the mid-1980s that the press dubbed his administration the 'Tanakasone Cabinet'.

Tanaka's health and influence ebbed in the late 1980s but the role of dirty money in Japanese politics kept going strong. In 1992, one of Tanaka's protégés, a man named Kanemaru Shin, was implicated in a bribery scandal involving a delivery company, the Inagawa-kai *yakuza* group and some 200 politicians. Kanemaru – nicknamed 'The Don' – was already notorious for playing pork-barrel politics, notably with Japan's construction industry, whose lobbying power was etched across the Japanese landscape in roads to nowhere, concrete river embankments and ugly concrete tetrapods strewn across beaches. Still, raids on his home in 1993 managed to top all that. Some $50 million was discovered, in everything from cash to gold bars. Stories circulated about how bribe money used to be wheeled through his office on trolleys, in full view of everyone: around $4 million in cash on one occasion.

Kanemaru died before his trial on charges of tax evasion could conclude, and the public was left without justice, just as Japan's economic fortunes were starting to falter. It was one thing to be lumbered with politicians who seemed constantly to be on the make, and with a main political party, the LDP, whose history was threaded through with dirty money and close relationships to organised crime. It was quite another for those same politicians to fail in their basic task of stewarding the wealth of the country at large. In 1993, Japan's postwar democracy showed signs of stirring from its slumber. The LDP, which had held power in Japan ever since its creation as a party in 1955, was at long last shown the door.

# CHAPTER 10

# Seeking 'Japan'

In January 1989, the longest imperial reign in Japanese history came to an end with the passing of Emperor Hirohito at the age of eighty-seven. Across more than six decades on the Chrysanthemum Throne, he had seen his country's modern experiment with democracy and internationalism collapse into authoritarianism and war, undergo radical rebirth during the Allied Occupation and take on a remarkable new form with Japan's rise to economic and technological superpower status.

And yet the accession of Hirohito's son Akihito, and the exchange of the old Shōwa reign-name for Heisei – 'achieving peace' – inspired mixed feelings in Japan. The death of Hirohito put the war firmly in the past, but the country's future appeared less certain than ever. For a brief period in 1988, the land around the imperial palace in Tokyo had been worth about the same as the whole of California: a symptom of a 'bubble economy' created in part by efforts, at the request of desperate western trading partners drowning in Japanese cars, cameras and televisions, to try to stimulate more demand within Japan for foreign goods.

Efforts by Japan's Ministry of Finance to deflate the bubble slowly by raising borrowing rates in late 1989 had the effect instead of bursting it. The Nikkei stock exchange lost half its value in the space of a year, and the real estate market collapsed under the weight of bad loans. Exports to the United States fell precipitously amid a rapid decline in the value of the dollar, and unemployment doubled to a postwar high of 5.4 per cent. Over the next thirty years, government debt as a percentage of GDP would rise from 60 per cent to a whopping 220 per cent as a succession of prime ministers – often at the rate of a new one every year – struggled to salvage the country's economic fortunes and global reputation.

Widespread use of the phrase 'lost decade' to describe Japan's predicament in the 1990s revealed just how central the story of rapid economic growth had become to perceptions of postwar Japan, both at home and abroad. That began to change as a contest heated up to redefine Japan's past. Its origins lay in the 1950s, when Occupation-era education reforms were rolled back and the Ministry of Education created a standardised school curriculum rooted in Japan's 'unique culture'. Private companies produced textbooks to match the curriculum, which Ministry bureaucrats then vetted, sometimes returning them with requests for edits. Treatment of the history of the 1930s and 1940s was especially sensitive, and from the 1980s onwards, textbook revisions began to make international headlines as Japan developed a reputation for falling far below the standard set by West Germany for coming to terms with its wartime past.

The first big flashpoint was an attempt, in 1982, to have school textbooks describe Japan's activities on the Asian mainland as an 'advance' (*shinshutsu*) rather than an 'invasion' (*shinnyū*). Outrage across East Asia was compounded three years later when Prime Minister Nakasone Yasuhiro paid an official visit, in full mourning dress, to Tokyo's Yasukuni Shrine. The shrine commemorated all Japan's modern war dead, including Nakasone's own brother, who had died in a kamikaze mission. But ever since it had become known, in 1978, that the souls of fourteen Class A war criminals had secretly been enshrined there, a convention had been observed whereby politicians visited in a personal capacity only or not at all. In 1986, Nakasone further upset foreign public opinion, this time in the United States, by claiming in a speech that Americans were less intelligent than Japanese because African Americans and Hispanics lowered the average.

Such ideas had become common in Japan over recent years, as a publishing trend for *nihonjinron* – 'theories about the Japanese' – took hold. These were attempts to explain Japan's remarkable postwar comeback in terms of supposedly unique aspects of Japanese people's biology, psychology, culture and values. Westerners had played their part in encouraging the trend. The wartime anthropologists Geoffrey Gorer and Ruth Benedict argued, respectively, that harsh toilet training helped explain Japan's culture of violence and that whereas westerners inhabited a 'guilt culture' – emphasising individual moral responsibility – the Japanese lived in a 'shame culture' where what mattered was the approbation of others.

Postwar psychologists and sociologists went on to paint the western – and in particular the American – psyche as the polar opposite of the Japanese. Americans were individualistic and egocentric, inclined towards competition and the building of strong personal stories. Japanese, by contrast, were said to thrive on community and co-operation, and to be well-attuned to the needs of others. There was, of course, some truth to this. But combined with the difficulty of the Japanese language, the country's relative inaccessibility to tourism and the enduring allure of Zen Buddhism, these ideas helped foster an inflated view in the West of Japan as a land of superior values and even mystical wisdom.

Across the 1980s and into the 1990s, assertions of Japanese cultural uniqueness helped to feed the idea that an unreasonably self-flagellating view of the Second World War had been implanted in young Japanese minds by Occupation education reforms – and must now be revised. One found the results in books like 'Nankin gyakusatsu' no kyokō (The Fabrication of the 'Nanjing Massacre', 1984) and in comments like those made by Nakasone's education minister, Fujio Masayuki, who downplayed the extent of the Nanjing Massacre and described Japan's colonisation of Korea as being more like a 'merger' sought by the Korean side. In 1989, the politician and novelist Ishihara Shintarō published The Japan That Can Say 'No': Why Japan Will Be First among Equals, in which he argued that the economic success enjoyed by some Asian nations of late was due in part to their time spent under Japanese rule.

The death of Emperor Hirohito had the effect of intensifying talk of the war, as the passing of their former commander-in-chief made it easier for ex-soldiers of the Imperial Japanese Army to speak up – some of whom did so explicitly to refute revisionist claims like those found in Fabrication. Victims and survivors, too, continued to come forward. In memoirs and interviews, former prisoners of war relived terrifyingly inhumane treatment at the hands of

Japanese soldiers who had regarded them as doubly despicable: not just enemies, but enemies who had chosen surrender over death. Up there with the best-known battles of the war were now atrocities like the Bataan Death March and the building of the Thai–Burma 'Death' railway, which together cost tens of thousands of lives.

In 1991, a Korean woman named Kim Hak-sun became the first survivor of the so-called 'comfort stations' – military brothels created by the Imperial Japanese Army – to go public about her ordeal. In her case and others, the Japanese court system began to pick up where the Tokyo Trials in 1946–8 had left off: weighing evidence and handing down rulings. These included confirmation that Korean and other women had been forced into sexual slavery during the war, that there had indeed been a massacre at Nanjing and that Unit 731 had been involved in biological warfare research in Manchukuo.

At the very highest levels in Japan, there was remorse. In 1992, Emperor Akihito became the first Japanese emperor ever to visit China. While there, he expressed his 'deep sorrow' over the 'severe suffering' inflicted on the people of China by the Japanese armed forces. A year later, Japan's new Prime Minister, Hosokawa Morihiro, weighed in. Descended from Konoe Fumimarō on his mother's side and no less a figure than Emperor Kanmu on his father's, he started his premiership at the head of an anti-LDP coalition with approval ratings in excess of 70 per cent. On a trip to South Korea in November 1993, Hosokawa apologised for Japanese colonialism and for the drafting of Korean women into sexual slavery for the military.

Less than a year later, Hosokawa was forced from office

by yet another political scandal. The LDP returned to power in an unlikely coalition with the Socialists, and on 15 August 1995 the Socialist Prime Minister, Murayama Tomiichi, marked the fiftieth anniversary of the end of the war with an apology – backed unanimously by his cabinet – for Japan's 'colonial rule and aggression'. Sadly for those in Japan who wished to put all this behind them, revisionism remained a stubborn feature of conservative politics. Just days before Murayama's statement, his education minister commented that 'invasion' or 'non-invasion' depended on 'how you think about it'. On the day of the Murayama statement itself, eight cabinet members visited Yasukuni Shrine.

These arguments about the past actions of the Japanese military were taking place against a backdrop of uncertainty for its Self-Defence Forces, as the end of the Cold War raised the question of what next for the US–Japan alliance. Early signs were unpromising. In 1991, the SDF found itself fighting a rearguard action against terrible international publicity when a decision to send money rather than troops during the Gulf War led to accusations that the Japanese preferred to throw cash at problems rather than take risks. American authorship of Japan's pacifist constitution appeared to be forgotten as anger tinged with envy at Japan's still-formidable economy inspired the slogan 'They pay in yen, we pay in blood!'

The SDF's approach to publicity up until now was summed up by one of its senior figures: 'The pheasant would not be shot, but for its cries.' Given worries within Japan and across East Asia about the resurgence of militarism, the most sensible course of action for the SDF had been to keep its head down. That policy, it was clear, had to change. The advertising giant Dentsū was enlisted, and the SDF gained their very own mascot: the cute and inoffensive Prince Pickles, whose story was told in a dedicated manga series. His father, the king of Paprika, declares that Pickles cannot succeed him unless he first goes out and learns the value of maintaining a defence force. A series of adventures ensues, involving a treasured ally – the Broccoli Kingdom – and an Evil Empire, in the course of which Pickles comes to appreciate that there can be no peace without a credible deterrent. In later instalments of the manga, we find Pickles travelling to far-away Japan to train with the SDF, fast-roping from a helicopter and posing for pictures with his new comrades.

While the SDF's domestic popularity gradually increased, Japan's civilian politicians continued to struggle to convince the electorate that they were up to the job. The country went through no fewer than twelve prime ministers between 1987 and 2001, as fresh factions and opposition political parties came and went. When the Great Hanshin-Awaji Earthquake struck Kobe in January 1995, killing more than 6,000 people and destroying 400,000 buildings, the authorities' preparedness was found wanting. Local *yakuza* somehow managed to set up soup kitchens before emergency supplies found their way in. A few months later, a doomsday cult called Aum Shinrikyō released sarin gas on the Tokyo subway, killing twelve commuters. The group's leader, Asahara Shōkō, counted the Vatican and the CIA among his enemies and predicted a forthcoming apocalypse: bizarre fantasies – so why, people wondered, had Japanese society deteriorated to the point where a man like this could attract intelligent young people to his cause and his commune?

A popular answer to that question was that postwar Japan had failed to provide a sense of national purpose beyond economic growth, and now even that purpose was gone. Young people in the 1990s and early 2000s were left with markedly worse employment prospects than their parents, to the point where many expected never to be able to afford to start a family. Cue a catastrophising trend in popular sociology: 'Freeters' would only work part-time and on a casual basis; *Niito*, from the British acronym NEET, were those 'Not in Education, Employment or Training'; 'Parasite singles' sponged off their parents and spent much of their time shopping; *Hikikomori* shut themselves away in their rooms for months or even years on end; and 'herbivorous men' homed in on hobbies and grooming at the expense of work and social relationships. Foreign media, especially, thrilled to stories of 'compensated dating': Japanese high school girls offering sexual favours to men old enough to be their fathers in return for the latest high-end accessories.

For all that Japan-watchers in the 1990s were tempted to conclude that the country was going to hell in a Louis Vuitton handbag, Japanese culture retained its time-honoured capacity to hold a fracturing polity together. At home, a combination of food, travel, literature, film, computer games, anime and manga helped to offset economic and political disappointments and anxieties. Abroad, many of these same features of Japanese life helped to generate warmth towards Japan despite the negative headlines about history wars and the country's declining *joie de vivre*.

Life expectancy in Japan in 1947 had been fifty-two. By

2005, it was over eighty, thanks in no small part to a diet that had remained substantially the same for hundreds of years. In contrast to the complexity of the fine French cuisine to be found in cities like Tokyo and Osaka, the rule with Japanese food was simple: high-quality ingredients, minimally cooked and minimally seasoned. Rice remained the nation's staple, often served with miso soup and pickles, alongside fish that was fresh enough to be eaten raw: on its own as sashimi, or with vinegared rice as sushi (the word possibly derived from *sui*, meaning 'sour'), with a little soy sauce and wasabi on the side. Since the Meiji era, beef had been back on the menu, too, valued at first for what was believed to be its physique-building and healing potential. Soldiers were fed it, the emperor tried it and soon cities like Tokyo were full of stew shops offering beef fried with various combinations of spring onions, miso, tofu, soy sauce and mirin (a sweet *sake*). Later, as Japan bounced back from the war, new and marginally less healthy culinary trends emerged, among them instant ramen, curry rice, fried chicken and spaghetti and pasta dishes.

Abroad, Japanese food had remained somewhat niche in the early postwar age: food for the counterculture young of the 1960s and their health-conscious successors in the 70s – if you were the sort to worry about processed food, nothing beat watching a sushi chef prepare your meal from scratch right in front of you. From the 1990s onwards, Japanese food, and sushi in particular, hit the big time across much of the West. Chain restaurants like Itsu and Yo! Sushi, both founded in 1997, helped to drive the boom onwards. In 2006, a Japanese government ministry went as far as certifying

Japanese restaurants abroad, to reassure customers that they knew what they were doing. The initiative was soon dubbed the 'sushi police', spawning a tongue-in-cheek anime by the same name.

The 1990s and 2000s also witnessed the onward global march of Japanese visual culture, now in a variety of new forms. It began with Space Invaders (1978) and Bubble Bobble (1986): arcade games which neither Murasaki Shikibu nor Tokugawa Ieyasu, had they taken a turn at the controls, would have recognised as meaningfully 'Japanese'. But these two titles, produced by Japan's Taito Corporation, heralded the age of the video game. By the mid-90s, games consoles produced by Nintendo and Sega featured in family fun and feuding the world over, making celebrities in the process of the Mario Brothers and Sonic the Hedgehog. In 1996, the Pokémon franchise got started on the Game Boy, and Miyazaki Hayao's Studio Ghibli signed a distribution deal with Disney, bringing some of Japan's most beloved animated films to wider western audiences, including *My Neighbour Totoro* (1988) and *Grave of the Fireflies* (1988). A new high was reached a few years later in 2003, when Miyazaki's *Spirited Away* won an Oscar.

By this time, Japanese fashion, too, was making its mark in the West. Issey Miyake was just a boy when the atom bomb was dropped on his home city of Hiroshima. He went on to study fashion in Tokyo and Paris before moving to New York, taking with him a taste for elegance over glamour and a sense of how a garment should allow the body to move that he credited to his study of the kimono. His best-known western client was Apple's Steve Jobs, who was so impressed by the uniform that Miyake created for Sony that he asked him to create uniforms for Apple staff, too. The idea went down badly in Cupertino, but Miyake went on to provide Jobs with his trademark black turtleneck. Rei Kawakubo and her Comme des Garçons label found success in the West, too, thanks to her transfer to modern fashion of Japan's *wabi-sabi* aesthetic: a look that feels artfully incomplete, worn and perishable.

Even critics of modern Japan found sympathetic audiences abroad. Magical, melancholy novels like *Norwegian Wood* (1987) turned Murakami Haruki into a literary superstar. In 1994, Kenzaburō Ōe, a fierce critic both of wartime ultra-nationalism and the 'confused and lost' state of post-war Japan, became the second Japanese writer after Kawabata Yasunari in 1968 to win the Nobel Prize for Literature. In the world of contemporary art, the Neo-pop artist Murakami Takashi gained worldwide attention for his vivid, manga-inspired work and his Superflat movement, which set out to satirise Japanese consumer culture. Both he and the artist Yayoi Kusama, famous for her polka-dot motif, came to be regarded as global rather than 'Japanese' artists.

Japan meanwhile continued to be a lucrative market for western mass culture, from Disney – Emperor Hirohito is rumoured to have been buried with his beloved Mickey Mouse watch – to rock bands like Bon Jovi and Radiohead. Fans of the latter in Osaka helped to place kindness and consideration on the list of western associations with Japan: worried that Radiohead's drummer Phil Selway was being overshadowed by the band's lead singer and guitarist, they decided to start a 'Phil Is Great' fan club.

By this point, Japan had a lively pop music scene of its own. A boom for big-band jazz, mambo and boogie-woogie during the Occupation was followed by a rockabilly craze – one performer, bending his legs and thrusting his guitar theatrically into the air, was described by a bemused critic as waddling across the stage 'like a child with polio'. The Beatles played the Budōkan in 1966, helping guitar music, from electric to folk, to shape much of the 1960s and 1970s in Japan.

Big names of the 1970s and 1980s included Hibari Misora, the undisputed 'Queen of Enka'. This was a type of sentimental ballad, often written in a *yonanuki* minor key – formed by removing the fourth (*yo*) and seventh (*na*) notes from its western minor counterpart – and heavily associated with nostalgia for a bygone Japan. A child star during the Occupation period, Hibari had gone on to become a postwar television icon: instantly recognisable on stage dressed in her kimono, hair coiffed, grasping a microphone and singing wistfully – sometimes with a tear in her eye – about lost loves and memories of old home towns. Joining Hibari on karaoke set-lists, as the technology began to take off, was the Yellow Magic Orchestra, starring the renowned composer Sakamoto Ryūichi on keyboards and vocals.

Hip-hop, reggae and R&B all enjoyed a strong presence in Japan, too, but the 1990s and 2000s belonged above all to the precision-tooled pop of boy- and girl-bands like SMAP and AKB48. The latter was formed in 2005 as a girl group whose members would split into teams to allow for daily performances in Tokyo's Akihabara district and for fans to meet their favourites. Western media developed an intense interest in some of the men, known as *otaku*, who spent much of their lives and income on meetings with 'idols' like these, alongside toys, games and memorabilia related to the fantasy worlds of manga and anime.

Television series like *Japanorama* (2002–7), presented by Jonathan Ross, helped to bring these strands of Japanese pop culture to ever-wider western audiences, often portraying the culture as weird: extreme, humorous and at once cute and worryingly sex-obsessed – the fact that similar anime techniques were used to create children's programmes and violent pornography appears to have confused audiences in the West. In the wider western media, stories about Japan increasingly gravitated towards the sensational: crazy technologies (toilets were a particular favourite), gruesome murders (overlooking Japan's ultra-low crime rates) and the despondent, sexless young.

More positively for Japan, the popularity of manga and anime among young people in China and Korea helped to counterbalance – at least to an extent – what they learned at school or over the family dinner table about the crimes of the Japanese Empire. The challenge for Japanese political leaders in the early twenty-first century was to offer a real-world account of 'Japan' that would be capable of inspiring confidence and attracting support both at home and abroad.

After a period spent changing prime ministers so rapidly that members of Bill Clinton's administration made a parlour game of trying to recall them all, along came a national leader in 2001 who was gifted with both star and staying power. Koizumi Junichirō of the LDP – known to his fans as 'Jun-chan' – served as prime minister for five years. During that time he wooed George W. Bush with his Elvis impressions, worked to reduce government debt and extended Nakasone's deregulation of the economy with policies that included the privatisation of Japan's postal service and encouragement of short-term contracts for workers. Having served the maximum term permitted under LDP rules at the time, Koizumi resigned in September 2006. There followed a return to revolving-door premierships until Abe Shinzō took up the post in 2012. He remained there until 2020, becoming the longest-serving prime minister in Japanese history and giving the country a clear sense of direction at last.

Abe came to power in the shadow of two recent traumas. The first was the 'Lehman Shock' of 2008. The collapse of the American financial services firm Lehman Brothers was felt keenly in Japan. Exports fell by nearly 40 per cent, unemployment rose to 5.5 per cent by mid-2009 – the result, in part, of Koizumi's loosening of the labour market – and five years of modest economic growth came to an abrupt end. In August 2009, the LDP was ejected from power and the Democratic Party of Japan (DPJ) replaced them. This was the first time since 1955 that a party other than the LDP had held a majority of seats in both houses of the Diet. It looked as though two-party politics in Japan might finally have become a reality. Unfortunately, Prime Minister Hatoyama Yukio was soon felled by a combination of yet another financial scandal and his failure to stand up to the United States over controversial plans to relocate one of its military bases in Okinawa. The islands had reverted to Japanese control in 1972, but the bases continued to be a source of anguish and anger among Okinawans.

Hatoyama was gone within a year, replaced by his minister of finance Kan Naoto. It was on Kan's watch that Japan suffered its second trauma. On 11 March 2011, the most powerful earthquake ever recorded in the country's history – magnitude 9 – struck off the coast of north-eastern Honshū. It was followed by a devastating tsunami, nearly forty metres high in places, which wiped out entire towns, killed around 20,000 people and triggered a meltdown at the Fukushima Dai-ichi nuclear power plant. So serious was the crisis in its early days, with a succession of hydrogen explosions causing ever-greater damage at the plant, that the possibility was briefly considered of evacuating Tokyo.

Amid widespread homelessness and conflicting claims about the risks of nuclear contamination, two of Japan's most important institutions won praise for their response. Emperor Akihito delivered a televised address offering solidarity and encouragement to the people of Japan. He and his wife Empress Michiko later visited evacuation shelters, dressing in casual clothes and chatting to people who had just lost everything. Meanwhile, the sight of around 100,000 soldiers from Japan's Self-Defence Forces rescuing people, clearing roads and delivering emergency supplies did far more for the SDF's status in Japanese society than Prince Pickles could ever have hoped to achieve.

The Japanese government's response to '3/11' quickly came in for severe criticism. Leaders at the time appeared deeply confused, inclined to downplay risks on the basis of little or even contradictory evidence, and within months were undermined by politicians jockeying for position within both the DPJ and the LDP. Prime Minister Kan ended up resigning, and after a brief stint by a DPJ successor, the LDP claimed power once again in December 2012 under Abe Shinzō.

Abe was the grandson of Kishi Nobusuke, who had been forced to resign his premiership over the Anpo protests of 1960. Back then, Kishi had enjoyed brief moments of respite by crawling around the floor with little Shinzō on his back, the latter shouting a slogan he had heard on the television: *'Anpo hantai! Anpo hantai!'* ('No to Anpo! No to Anpo!'). As prime minister, Abe very much shared his grandfather's politics. He was a nationalist who was impatient both with guilt-inducing approaches to the past and with those who sought a perpetual pacifism for Japan. He established a National Security Council to centralise security policy, expanded the armed forces with drone and amphibious capabilities, supported a new stance of collective self-defence – allowing the SDF to come to the aid of an ally if Japan itself were ultimately in danger – and promised that henceforth Japan would seek to make 'proactive contributions to peace'.

To Abe's detractors, this last sounded like a euphemism. But in practice it meant the strengthening of Japan's multilateral relationships in the Asia-Pacific, with the aim of balancing out China's rise as the region's preeminent power. China had overtaken Japan in 2010 as the world's second-largest economy and it remained vital to Japan as a trading partner. With that in mind, Abe worked to improve Sino-Japanese relations while also making clear his support for Taiwan. As he put it in 2021, a year after stepping down as prime minister: 'A Taiwan emergency is a Japanese emergency, and therefore an emergency for the US–Japan alliance. People in Beijing,

President Xi in particular, should never have a misunderstanding in recognising this.' So important to Abe was the US–Japan relationship that in November 2016 he raced to become the first foreign leader to meet President-elect Donald Trump. During President Trump's first term in office, the pair sometimes spoke as often as twice per week on the phone.

At home, Abe attempted to get the Japanese economy going again with a 'three arrow' strategy of quantitative easing, stimulus spending and structural reforms. The IMF judged 'Abenomics' a modest success in 2017, but most commentators declared it a failure in the end: economic growth was disappointing and Abe's hope of raising inflation to 2 per cent – in order to boost business profits and help the economy to heat up – remained out of reach. Nor was there a solution in sight to one of Japan's greatest challenges: a predicted population decline from 128 million in 2010 to just 83 million in 2100, with a third of the population expected to be over the age of sixty-five by 2040.

Attempts to get more women into the workforce – dubbed 'womenomics' – succeeded in terms of overall numbers but foundered on a lack of childcare and an enduring failure in Japan to match other advanced economies in the number of women occupying senior roles. On the question of migration, considered essential to provide enough care workers and taxpayers to look after Japan's elderly population, the general public had yet to be convinced that the influx of large numbers of people would be a better solution than the 'care-bot' technology under development in both Japan and China.

*

Those inclined to connect changes in Japan's ancient imperial institution with the country's wider fortunes looked forward to great things on 1 May 2019, as Japan entered another new era. Emperor Akihito took the rare step of abdicating the throne, on grounds of physical frailty, and his son Naruhito took his place. The new reign name chosen was Reiwa, 'beautiful harmony'. Supporters of Japan's monarchy found cause for optimism in the fact that Naruhito and his wife Masako were the first emperor and empress to be born after the war and to have benefited from a university education. Naruhito had studied at Oxford University, while Masako had passed through Harvard and Tokyo on her way to winning a coveted position in the Ministry of Foreign Affairs.

Loath to leave behind her career, Masako had responded to Naruhito's first proposal of marriage by asking whether it was permitted for her to turn him down. Naruhito countered that there was much for an aspiring diplomat like Masako to achieve from within the imperial family. Masako relented, agreeing to marry him and plunging herself into the 'Princess Education': a crash-course in the ancient arts of the imperial court, from calligraphy to *waka* poetry. The couple's wedding, in June 1993, was no less rich in tradition. It had taken place at the Imperial Sanctuary: a simple, cedarwood shrine within the grounds of the imperial palace in Tokyo, dedicated to the sun goddess Amaterasu. Masako underwent a ritual bath before being dressed in a twelve-layered garment, its outermost layer crafted from green and gold silk. Naruhito offered a sacred *sakaki* branch to the gods, pledged to take care of Masako and the two sealed the ceremony with sips of *sake*.

The wedding ceremony was part of the imperial mystique

that Naruhito and Masako were now required to preserve as emperor and empress. Masako at times struggled. In centuries past, the imperial family had learned to live at the mercy of shoguns and warlords. Their masters now were the staff of the Imperial Household Agency, some of whom regarded Masako as an interloper: a commoner whose personality had been warped by time spent in America and whose fluency in conversation with foreign leaders risked overshadowing her husband. Masako ended up fulfilling the constitutional role of 'symbol of the nation' by becoming one of Japan's most high-profile sufferers from depression, as the limitations on her life and the pressure to produce an heir became too much. The birth of a child, Princess Aiko, in December 2001 had done little to alleviate that pressure. Under rules created in the Meiji era and retained during the Occupation, only men could ascend the Chrysanthemum Throne. As things stood, the throne would one day pass from Naruhito to his brother Prince Akishino. The Japanese media went from celebrating the imperial match as Japan's answer to Charles and Diana to reporting rumours that Masako was allowing her husband to shoulder alone the burden of their imperial duties while she shopped and ate in upmarket restaurants with her friends.

Here, in microcosm, was the debate raging between Japanese social critics from the 1990s into the 2010s. Were psychological and social problems on the rise because of thwarted opportunities, as the economy continued to struggle? Or was the economy struggling because too many Japanese no longer possessed the optimism, clarity of purpose and nation-building mettle of their Meiji and postwar forebears?

Those who saw in Abe Shinzō a solution to dilemmas

like these, as a leader of rare vision despite the corruption allegations that alongside long-standing health problems, led him to resign in August 2020, were left in shock and mourning on 8 July 2022 when he was shot dead while out campaigning for an LDP colleague in the ancient city of Nara. The man suspected of killing Abe said that he had shot him because of his support for the Unification Church, which had taken large donations from his mother and left the family in poverty as a result. In the weeks after Abe's death, popular support for the Japanese cabinet fell as the general public learned the extent of LDP politicians' support for the church, which was founded in South Korea in 1954 by Sun Myung Moon and was known for mass weddings among its members – who were often referred to as 'Moonies'.

Religion and state were kept separate from one another under Japan's postwar constitution, and by the early twenty-first century most Japanese treated religion as part of the country's rich cultural weave rather than maintaining any particular commitments. The phrase 'born Shintō, die Buddhist' captured it well: Shintō provided ritual support in pregnancy, after a birth and during the stages of childhood, while funerals and memorials were usually conducted in Buddhist temples. A great many Japanese added a Christian element to their lives by having a western-style church wedding at which a priest – sometimes ordained, sometimes a foreigner who looked the part and needed the money – would officiate.

And yet this was not the whole story. Postwar Japan was home to a range of 'new religions' derived mostly from Shintō and Buddhism, among the most powerful of which was Sōka Gakkai ('Value Creation Society'), rooted in the teachings of Nichiren. By the end of the 1960s, Sōka Gakkai claimed around 7 million members, some of whom founded a centre-right political party called Kōmeitō. Sōka Gakkai and Kōmeitō officially separated in 1970 after claims that they were violating the constitution. But they retained deep connections nonetheless, and from 1999 onwards Kōmeitō frequently entered into coalition with the LDP. The Unification Church was far less influential in Japan, but Abe's grandfather Kishi Nobusuke was said to have established ties with his fellow conservative Sun Myung Moon in an effort to build support for the LDP and to combat communism and the influence of trades unions. His grandson, it seemed, had now paid a high price for that relationship.

For millions of Japanese who felt disillusioned with their politicians, a popular solution was to volunteer or join one of Japan's many non-profit organisations (NPOs), either working collaboratively with the state or putting pressure on it. Causes included cleaning streets, campaigning for the environment, supporting the elderly and helping the people of north-eastern Honshū to return to some semblance of normal life after 3/11. Another way forward, when national politicians couldn't or wouldn't back your cause, was to put more energy into local government. Campaigners across the 2010s succeeded in persuading local administrations to offer official status to same-sex couples, while waiting for the LDP to change its mind on the issue. By 2024, public opinion was strongly in favour of allowing same-sex marriages, and a number of district courts declared Japan's ban to be unconstitutional.

Just as a phrase like 'lost decades' revealed too narrow an

emphasis on the economy within Japanese life, so the idea that the country's affairs ought to be shaped by an iron triangle of politicians, civil servants and big business was beginning to feel past its best. Back in the Meiji and Taishō eras, a certain public-spiritedness had been deemed essential to Japan's success in the world: in 1909, the journalist Ishikawa Hanzan had proudly announced that the cause of a recent nervous collapse had been his membership of 100 governmental and social organisations. Few Japanese, either then or in the 2020s, would push themselves quite that hard. But there was a recognition now that Japan's economic and demographic challenges – in 2024, Japan slipped below Germany to become only the world's fourth-largest economy – would inevitably mean a steady reduction in what the state could do. One possible future for democracy in Japan involved ever more citizens choosing a cause or causes, giving up some time and money and doing deals with business and government where required; side-stepping their much-maligned political class and forging 'Japan' for themselves.

# Epilogue

A family sits around a hearth of burning logs, sunk into the floor, with a simple cast-iron pot suspended overhead. Green tatami mats, freshly laid and fragrant, stretch out towards the thick wooden columns and sliding partitions of bare wood and white paper that mark the boundaries of this main room in the house. Smoke rises upwards past blackened cypress beams, through a roof thatched with rice-straw – helping to keep it dry and insect-free – and outwards from there into a wintry night.

A *minka* – 'folk house' – like this represents a gathering-in of all that surrounds it: cypress, pine, cedar and camphor; grasses, rushes and reeds. It would once have been a chilly prospect at this time of the year. No more. Concealed behind the wood-and-paper screens are triple-glazed windows. The tatami mats are heated from underneath. Over in one corner, a cylinder of *washi* (Japanese paper) conceals a fire extinguisher while in another a cabinet of lacquered wood keeps a wi-fi router and various other gadgets discreetly out of sight.

Attempts to reverse postwar migration trends in Japan, which have created overstuffed mega-cities and left hollowed-out 'ghost villages' in their wake, hinge on making rural Japan a more enticing prospect. Members of a growing *minka* movement are doing their bit by restoring traditional homes while adding in a few modern comforts. Family scenes like this one, members gathered around a rural hearth, may become more common thanks to generous government subsidies for those who exchange urban for rural living. Japanese may be persuaded to brave a relative lack of schools, healthcare and work opportunities, not to mention a sparse cultural calendar, for the sake of a healthier and more laid-back pace of life. Visitors to Japan may choose homes like these, too, while they take a few days' break from the tourist trail. Migrants fleeing skyrocketing living costs elsewhere in the world might find themselves likewise attracted to Japan's countryside, benefiting from lower land and house prices and staying for months or years at a time on company or new 'digital nomad' visas.

For all that *minka* renovations have become a serious business of late, not least on social media, where video diaries earn millions of hits by tracing a property's journey from dilapidation to dream home, the turning of the urban migration tide remains a distant prospect. Tourism to Japan is meanwhile booming, but at the cost of more and more stories about visitors falling short of Japanese standards on noise, litter and behaviour. Migration to Japan, too, is on the rise, largely from Asian countries including China, Vietnam and South Korea. And yet, although Japanese public opinion is largely in favour of it – western stereotypes about Japanese xenophobia are badly out of date – the country has yet to produce a leader who is able or brave enough to make a coherent, compelling case for the kind of change that Japan needs in order to weather its demographic crisis. Where next, then, for Japan?

As with a home, so with a history. The story of Japan has been one of a great gathering-in of resources: people and ideas from across the archipelago, from mainland Asia and latterly from all around the world. The forming and re-forming of all this into something called 'Japan', across many centuries, has depended as much on a sympathetic awareness of the past as on grand plans for the future. The gods, the emperor, Tokugawa Ieyasu, the Meiji-era founding fathers, one's old home town: the rhetoric of return to something glorious or simply something decent has proven powerful, time and again. Writers and artists in the twentieth century variously sought Japan in the aroma given off by Jōmon-era earthenware, in *boromono* – clothes stitched together from recycled rags – in train trips to revered historical sights, in the silence of ancient forests and in the folklore of people written off as backward but whose wisdom was said to run deeper than any formal education.

Comparatively few, of late, have sought Japan in Korea. But perhaps it is time they did, taking a lesson from Emperor Akihito, who in 2001 commented on his descent, via Emperor Kanmu, from a Korean king. Late-twentieth-century history wars and worries about China's rise to pre-eminence in the Asia-Pacific region have tended to overshadow just how much Japan, Korea and China share in common: not least a long cultural history and a range of contemporary challenges including ageing and shrinking populations. For all his faults, Prime Minister Tanaka Kakuei was surely on to something when he sat with Mao Zedong and discussed Buddhism, Confucianism and incense.

The mixed origins of Japanese culture – in China, Korea and the wider world, alongside the archipelago itself – have not prevented that culture from serving as the glue that holds the country together during periods of political turmoil. Sometimes it has been strategically deployed, by social climbers at home – from medieval warlords to early-modern merchants – or by diplomats abroad. Most of the time, however, Japanese culture has flourished simply by people enjoying it, as they do now around the country in countless clubs dedicated to sport, martial arts and various fine and performing arts, not to mention standing around in Japan's ubiquitous *konbini* – twenty-four-hour convenience stores – flicking through books of manga.

Perhaps culture will be called into service once again in the decades to come, as Japan's demographic crisis forces a shift from the ethnic nationalism of the past to a civic nationalism that can fully incorporate newcomers. The fear otherwise is that fifty years from now Japan will be split between a dwindling native population, a poorly paid underclass of migrants mostly from South-East Asia and a corps of AI-powered care-bots – although despite the techno-optimism of the 2010s, the latter have yet to emerge as a viable solution to Japan's problems.

Recent years have seen tentative moves towards a civic nationalism for Japan, not least in the steady reversal of twentieth-century attempts to suppress minority cultures such as those of the Ainu, Zainichi Koreans (people of Korean descent living in Japan) and the people of the

Ryūkyū Islands. Had Tokyo's hosting of the Summer Olympics for the second time in 2021 not been so compromised by COVID-19, more foreign visitors might have travelled to see the Upopoy National Ainu Museum in Hokkaidō: a major new centre for the research and preservation of Ainu heritage. Regionalism in general remains strong in Japan. For most of its past, the archipelago has been a patchwork of communities, only loosely tied to some nominal centre like Kyoto. Postwar trends point in a similar direction: towards volunteering and getting things done in partnership with local government when national politicians disappoint.

A darker possibility in the medium term is that Japan's domestic travails end up paling in comparison to its international ones. Worries about China, Russia and North Korea are intensifying, and calls are growing for the Self-Defence Forces to be permitted a means of pre-emptively destroying missile launch facilities abroad rather than relying on missile defence – a spear to go alongside the shield. Meanwhile, the sun-seekers and scuba divers who usually flock to Japan's far south-western islands nearest Taiwan are being joined by SDF personnel sent to man radar stations. The prospect looms of the US–Japan security alliance, so controversial since the end of the Occupation, failing just when it is needed: when China's military capabilities have grown and American interest in Taiwan has declined to the point where a Chinese attempt to take the island by force becomes feasible – potentially with the capture of some of Japan's south-western islands along the way, for use as forward operating bases.

Perhaps in the end, the self-interest of China's leaders, not least when it comes to the value of trade with Japan, the

United States and its South-East Asian neighbours, will help to steer the region in a more peaceful direction than most analysts currently expect. Should that happen, it is possible to imagine China and Japan becoming a powerful co-operative force in the world, working together in a range of areas from the advancement and regulation of AI to the pioneering of technological solutions to climate change. Given the great apprehension and misunderstanding of China in the West, the Chinese might learn from Japan a little about the workings of soft power: how the arts, reasonably free of government control, can help in sharing something of ordinary Chinese life and the country's creative imagination with people around the world.

Whatever happens in and to Japan during the years to come we can hope that growing interest in its history among tourists and Japanophiles will help to keep alive Japanese people's pride in and understanding of their own rich and varied past. It remains, as ever, a mine of good ideas for the future, a source of consolation during hard times and an inspiration for all those who call this fertile archipelago home.

# Acknowledgements

For seeding and supporting my interest in Japan, I owe a debt of gratitude to Teikyo UK and the Daiwa Anglo-Japanese Foundation. Teikyo trusted me to tour wonderful groups of visiting Japanese students around the UK and Europe. Daiwa gave me the opportunity to live, study and work in Japan: the first of a number of happy periods spent living and working there. At the University of Edinburgh, I continue to cherish the company and conversation of colleagues and students alike, whose enthusiasm for Japanese history is a constant source of inspiration. At BBC Radio, I have had the chance to explore all sorts of aspects of Japanese life – from jazz to the supernatural – thanks to opportunities and pearls of editorial wisdom that have come my way courtesy of, amongst others, Robyn Read, Hugh Levinson, Matthew Dodd, Fiona McLean and Luke Mulhall. Thank you to everyone at Northbank Talent Management, especially my agent Matthew Cole, and to all at Penguin who helped to bring this book into being: my editor Simon Winder and copy-editor Robert Sharman, alongside Anna Tuck and Lotte Hall. To my wife, Kae: thank you for your love, support and patient willingness to participate in the occasional one-woman survey of Japanese public opinion. And to my children, Shoji, Yocchan and Hana: what a joy it was to encounter the magic of Japanese pop culture through your infant eyes. Would that I could turn the clock back and live that all again.

# Bibliographic Notes

On the natural history of the Japanese archipelago, see Conrad Totman's *A History of Japan* (Wiley, 2000). For ancient Japan, see Tatsuo Kobayashi, *Jōmon Reflections: Forager Life and Culture in the Prehistoric Japanese Archipelago* (2004; edited by Simon Kaner with Oki Nakamura); J. Edward Kidder, *Himiko and Japan's Elusive Chiefdom of Yamatai: Archaeology, History and Mythology* (University of Hawaii Press, 2007); Karl F. Friday (ed.), *Japan Emerging: Premodern History to 1850* (Routledge, 2018); Herman Ooms, *Imperial Politics and Symbolics in Ancient Japan: The Tenmu Dynasty, 650–800* (University of Hawaii Press, 2008); Bjarke Frellesvig, *A History of the Japanese Language* (Cambridge University Press, 2010); Michael I. Como, *Shōtoku: Ethnicity, Ritual, and Violence in the Japanese Buddhist Tradition* (Oxford University Press, 2008); Ross Bender, 'The Hachiman Cult and the Dōkyō Incident', *Monumenta Nipponica* 34/2 (1979). For a translation of and introduction to the Kokinshū poetry anthology, see Torquil Duthie, *The Kokinshū: Selected Poems* (Columbia University Press, 2023).

On Heian Japan, see Ivan Morris, *The World of the Shining Prince: Court Life in Ancient Japan* (Alfred A. Knopf, 1964); H. Paul Varley, *Japanese Culture* (University of Hawaii Press, 2000); Karl F. Friday (ed.), op. cit.; Jennifer Guest, 'Heian Japan' in Christopher Harding (ed.), *The Oxford Illustrated History of Japan*

(Oxford University Press, forthcoming). For medieval and early modern Japan, see Stephen Turnbull, *The Book of the Samurai* (Arco, 1982) and *The Mongol Invasions of Japan, 1274 and 1281* (Osprey, 2010); John Dougill, *Kyoto: A Cultural History* (Oxford University Press, 2005); Ronald P. Toby, *Engaging the Other: 'Japan' and its Alter-Egos, 1550–1850* (Brill, 2019); Mary Elizabeth Berry, *Hideyoshi* (Harvard University Press, 1982); Marius Jansen, *The Making of Modern Japan*, (paperback edition, Harvard University Press, 2002); Kenneth Henshall, *A History of Japan: From Stone Age to Superpower* (third edition, Palgrave Macmillan, 2012); Ivan Morris, *The Nobility of Failure: Tragic Heroes in the History of Japan* (Penguin, 1980); Morton S. Schmorleitz, *Castles in Japan* (Charles E. Tuttle Co., 1974); Robert Hellyer, 'Japan Reunited: The Early Modern Era' in Harding (ed.), op. cit.; Susan B. Hanley, *Everyday Things in Premodern Japan: The Hidden Legacy of Material Culture* (University of California Press, 1999); Christine M.E. Guth, *Craft Culture in Early Modern Japan: Materials, Makers, and Mastery* (University of California Press, 2021); Ihara Saikaku and Ivan Morris, *Life of An Amorous Woman and Other Writings* (New Directions, 1969); Matsunosuke Nishiyama and Gerald Groemer (translator), *Edo Culture: Daily Life and Diversions in Urban Japan, 1600–1868* (University of Hawaii Press, 1997); Naomichi Ishige, 'Food Culture' in Yoshio Sugimoto (ed.), *The Cambridge Companion to Modern Japanese Culture* (Cambridge University Press, 2009); Donald Keene, *Four Major Plays of Chikamatsu* (Columbia University Press, 1997); David Landis Barnhill (translator and introduction), *Bashō's Journey: The Literary Prose of Matsuo Bashō* (SUNY Press, 2005).

On modern and contemporary Japan, see Christopher Harding, *Japan Story: In Search of a Nation, 1850 to the Present* (Allen Lane,

2018); Simon Partner, 'The Birth of Modern Japan (1853–1931)' in Christopher Harding (ed.), *The Oxford Illustrated History of Japan* (Oxford University Press, forthcoming); Hugh Cortazzi, *Victorians in Japan: In and around the Treaty Ports* (Bloomsbury Academic, 2012); Marius Jansen, *The Making of Modern Japan* (paperback edition, Harvard University Press, 2002); Andrew Gordon, *A Modern History of Japan* (Oxford University Press, 2013); Christopher Harding, 'Kawanabe Kyōsai: The Demon With a Brush', *Royal Academy Magazine* (March 2022); Naoko Shimazu, *Japan, Race and Equality: The Racial Equality Proposal of 1919* (Routledge, 1998). Frederick R. Dickinson, *World War I and the Triumph of a New Japan* (Cambridge University Press, 2013); Urs Matthias Zachmann (ed.), *Asia after Versailles: Asian Perspectives on the Paris Peace Conference and the Interwar Order* (Edinburgh University Press, 2017); Kenneth Pyle, *The Making of Modern Japan* (second edition, Houghton Mifflin, 1995); Malcolm D. Kennedy, *The Estrangement of Great Britain and Japan, 1917–35* (Manchester University Press, 1969); Gary J. Bass, *Judgement at Tokyo: World War II on Trial and the Making of Modern Asia* (Knopf Publishing Group, 2023); Perry R. Hinton, *The Japanese in the Western Mind* (Routledge, 2023); Jing Sun, *Japan and China as Charm Rivals: Soft Power in Regional Diplomacy* (University of Michigan Press, 2012); Sabine Frühstück, *Uneasy Warriors: Gender, Memory, and Popular Culture in the Japanese Army* (University of California Press, 2007); Bonnie English, *Japanese Fashion Designers* (Bloomsbury, 2011); Ai Tsuneyoshi, 'The Changing Relationship Between the Non-Profit Sector and the State in Japan: Case Studies of NPOs in Fukushima', *Voluntas* 35 (2024). The poem beginning 'Spring has come' is attributed to Kamo no Taruhito (see *The Manyōshū: One Thousand Poems Selected and Translated from the Japanese*, Iwanami Shoten, 1940). The words of the oracle sought by Empress Shōtoku are found in Ross Bender, 'The Hachiman Cult and the Dōkyō Incident', *Monumenta Nipponica* 34/2 (1979). Excerpts from Sei Shōnagon's *Pillow Book* come from Ivan Morris's translation (*The Pillow Book of Sei Shōnagon*, Penguin, 1967). Excerpts from the *Kokinshū* come from Torquil Duthie, *The Kokinshū: Selected Poems* (Columbia University Press, 2023). Genshin's vision of the Pure Land appears in Paul H. Varley, Japanese Culture (University of Hawai'i Press, 2000). Excerpts from *The Tale of the Heike* come from the translation by Royall Tyler (*The Tale of the Heike*, Penguin, 2012). Saigyō's poetry features in Varley, op cit. Excerpts from *The Love Suicides at Sonezaki* come from Donald Keene, *Four Major Plays of Chikamatsu* (Columbia University Press, 1997). Excerpts from Matsuo Bashō's *The Narrow Road to the Deep North* (*Oku no Hosomichi*) come from David Landis Barnhill, *Bashō's Journey: The Literary Prose of Matsuo Bashō* (SUNY Press, 2005). The words of Mortimer Menpes, on Kyōsai, come from Mortimer Menpes, *Japan: A Record in Colour* (The Macmillan Company, 1901). 'Oh my brother . . .' is an excerpt from Yosano Akiko's poem '*Kimi, shinitamō koto nakare*' ['Brother, Do Not Offer Your Life'] (1904). The translation used here appears in Steve Rabson, 'Akiko on War: To Give One's Life or Not: A Question of Which War', *Journal of the Association of Teachers of Japanese*, 25:1 (1991). 'Admiral Tōgō possesses . . .' comes from Natsume Sōseki, *Wagahai wa neko de aru* ['I am a Cat'] (1905–1906), reproduced in P. N. Dale, *The Myth of Japanese Uniqueness* (Croom Helm, 1986).  ·

# Index

PELICAN BOOKS

PELICAN BOOKS

**Islam:**
**The Essentials**
Tariq Ramadan

**Basic Income:**
**And How We Can Make It Happen**
Guy Standing

**Think Like an Anthropologist**
Matthew Engelke

**Hermeneutics:**
**Facts and Interpretation in the Age of Information**
John D. Caputo

**Being Ecological**
Timothy Morton

**Object-Oriented Ontology:**
**A New Theory of Everything**
Graham Harman

**Marx and Marxism**
Gregory Claeys

**The Human Planet:**
**How We Created the Anthropocene**
Simon L. Lewis and Mark A. Maslin

**Think Again:**
**How to Reason and Argue**
Walter Sinnott-Armstrong

**Parenting the First Twelve Years:**
**What the Evidence Tells Us**
Victoria L. Cooper, Heather Montgomery, Kieron Sheehy

 PELICAN BOOKS

**PELICAN BOOKS**

Architecture:
From Prehistory to Climate Emergency
Barnabas Calder

Covid by Numbers:
Making Sense of the Pandemic with Data
David Spiegelhalter and Anthony Masters

Around the World in 80 Books
David Damrosch

How Religion Evolved:
And Why It Endures
Robin Dunbar

The Blue Commons:
Rescuing the Economy of the Sea
Guy Standing

The Holocaust:
An Unfinished History
Dan Stone

Aristotle:
Understanding the World's Greatest Philosopher
John Sellars

The Power of Language:
Multilingualism, Self and Society
Viorica Marian

Traditionalism:
The Radical Project for Restoring Sacred Order
Mark Sedgwick

 PELICAN BOOKS

The Politics of Time:
Gaining Control in the Age of Uncertainty
Guy Standing

Moral AI:
And How We Get There
Jana Schaich Borg, Walter Sinnott-Armstrong and
Vincent Conitzer

Race and Education:
Reproducing White Supremacy in Britain
Kalwant Bhopal

Understanding Media:
Communication, Power and Social Change
James Curran and Joanna Redden

Why War?
Richard Overy